Stewart Odendhal, DVM, PhD was born in San Diego but spent his formative years in Oklahoma City after his family returned when he was 2 years old, while his father, a U.S. Navy pilot, was often away on daring missions like the search for Amelia Earhart. After high school, Stewart ventured to UCLA for a biology B.A. in 1960, then studied veterinary science across state at UC Davis, receiving his DVM in 1967. The prestigious Johns Hopkins School of Public Health next tapped him to study foreign animal diseases in India.

This book is dedicated to my half-sister, Chrissy Odend'hal, who died on October 5, 2020 at 66 years old in Chico, California due to 'Complications of Chronic Alcoholism'.

And to my firstborn son, Philip Sherlock Odend'hal, who died at 55 years old, in Manly, Australia on December 14, 2017, due to an extra dose of heroin he did not even ask for.

Stewart Odendhal, DVM, PhD

I Have a Beautiful Brain, Compared to the Brains of Alcoholics and Drug Addicts

A Sincere Attempt to Reduce the Attractiveness of Alcohol for Children, Teenagers, and Young Adults

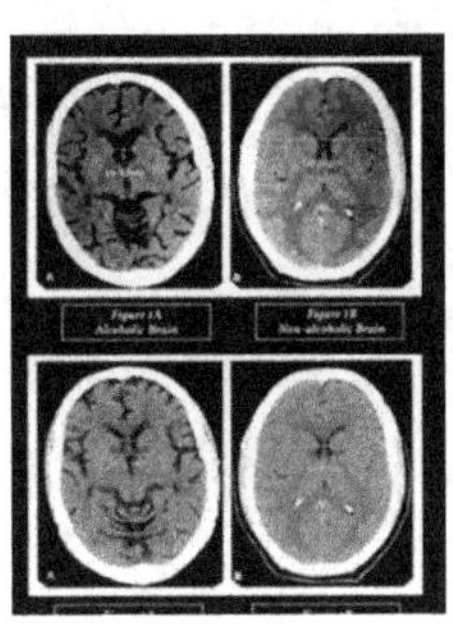

AUSTIN MACAULEY PUBLISHERS™

LONDON • CAMBRIDGE • NEW YORK • SHARJAH

Ordering Information
Quantity sales: Special discounts are available on quantity purchases by corporations, associations, and others. For details, contact the publisher at the address below.

Publisher's Cataloging-in-Publication data
Odendhal, DVM, PhD, Stewart
I Have a Beautiful Brain, Compared to the Brains of Alcoholics and Drug Addicts

ISBN 9798889109891 (Paperback)
ISBN 9798889109907 (Hardback)
ISBN 9798889109914 (ePub e-book)

Library of Congress Control Number: 2023922828

www.austinmacauley.com/us

First Published 2024
Austin Macauley Publishers LLC
40 Wall Street, 33rd Floor, Suite 3302
New York, NY 10005
USA

mail-usa@austinmacauley.com
+1 (646) 5125767

In particular, I want to thank the two authors that wrote the following academic article:

- Sandhu, Gurpreet S., and Hiresh R. Nagrale. "Computed Tomography Evaluation of Brain in Chronic Alcoholics." *Journal of Neurosciences in Rural Practice* 11 (2019): 63– 71. https://doi.org/10.1055/s-0039-1700610.

The publisher, Georg Thieme Verlag, provided permission for the use of the CT Brain Scan figures in this book.

Also, I wish to thank all of my family members, friends, and neighbors who expressed interest in the project and gave me encouragement during the project. In particular, my older brother, Charles Joseph Odend'hal III, and Baba Creelman and her husband Bill deserves gold stars for their editing and valuable suggestions. My lifelong friend, Don Chery, provided several excellent ideas.

Table of Contents

Appendixes

Chapter One
Prologue

Following a Computed Tomography (CT) scan of my head in order to rule out a possible cerebral hematoma, my wife, Marta, told me that the technician had said, as he looked at my radiograph, that I had a 'beautiful brain'. When the technician came out of the observation room, I asked him. "Did you tell my wife that I had a beautiful brain?"

"Yes, I did," he replied without any hesitation.

"Why did you say that?" I pleasantly inquired.

"Because it was clear to me that you were not an alcoholic or a drug user," he said, smiling back at me.

"Well, how could you possibly know that?" was my response.

He then said, "Oh, my, that's easy. I have been doing this same job for 40 years and all I have to do is just glance at the CT brain scan of anyone and if I see large spaces of brain tissue missing, I know immediately that that person will turn out to be either an alcoholic or a drug addict when the radiologists write their reports."

I thought to myself, *I didn't know that, and I wondered if alcoholics and drug addicts knew that.* If they did not know that; they certainly should. What about the general public? Are they aware of this possible situation or does this condition only affect the heavy alcohol users? How can I corroborate the technician's statement? Thus, a small tiny spot, somewhere in the depth of my beautiful brain called "curiosity" was suddenly mobilized and I just had to find out as much as I could about alcohol's effects on brain tissue and other relevant information.

After months and months of study, going to Alcoholics Anonymous (AA) meetings on two different continents, and talking with alcoholics, I have become interested in possible plans to improve the impact of the common knowledge of brain fragility on alcoholics and the public at large. This is particularly important in discouraging children, teenagers, and young adults from initiating any alcohol consumption. Chapters two and six present specific ideas toward these goals.

Chapter three deals with the experiences I have had with two alcoholic stepfathers and one alcoholic stepmother. My eldest son died of an over-dose of heroin at the age of 55 in December 2017, in Australia, and my youngest half-sister died at 66 years old, directly due to alcoholism in 2020; she died of esophageal varices rupture and bled to death.

Chapter four deals with the effects of alcohol on the brain and new scientific information regarding neurogenesis, glymphatic, and the shrinkage of supportive cells in the brain during sleep. All three of these informative research activities are fascinating things for me to read about and they may have a direct possible impact concerning the cessation of drinking alcohol, and thus, reduce the premature deaths of heavy-use alcoholics.

Chapter six covers my own addiction to smoking and the chance exposure at the University of California medical school in San Francisco with displays of smoking and non-smoking lungs. This turned the tide (so to speak) and convinced me never to ever smoke again (with one tiny momentary exception years later in India).

Chapter six takes up the tremendously important question of how to protect our children, teenagers, and other young adults from their first drink of alcohol, as well as how to influence alcohol users to grasp the life-or-death peril they could face if they do not stop drinking alcohol.

The Epilogue reviews the main themes of the book and speculates on the future activity to educate the general population of the spread of the dangers of remaining ignorant of the adverse effects of alcohol on the brains of alcoholics.

From time to time, I intend to include very short segments in the text, which at first appearance may seem unrelated to the major message of the book, but should either be entertaining, educational, or enlightening.

When I was 47 years old, my mother told me, "Stewart, when are you ever going to learn that not everybody thinks the way you do?"

To this inquiry, I replied with a glint in my eye, "I don't know when. But, what do you suppose is wrong with all of those who do not think the way I do?"

All kidding aside, I do have an appreciation for other cultures that think differently, both in certain parts of the United States of America and in foreign cultures around the world, having traveled extensively and conducted public health research on a daily basis while living in India, China,

Haiti, Italy, Kenya, Czech Republic, and Slovakia. I have served as a 'language editor' for a European scientific journal for many years and continue to do so presently. My research interests have been supported by grants from the National Institute of Health, the National Academy of Sciences, the National Science Foundation, the National Geographic Society, the Stanford Research Institute, the United States Fish and Wildlife Service, the Indo-U.S. Sub-Commission on Education and Culture, two senior Fulbright Fellowships to India, the Ford Foundation, the University of Georgia Research Foundation, and the Florida Game and Fresh-Water Fish Commission. My publications in peer-reviewed scientific journals include: geography, epidemiology, immunology, anatomy, diving physiology, demographic studies in India and China, ecological energetics in Indian and Chinese cattle, histochemical localization of specific immune cells in tissue sections, and cattle diseases in India (foot and mouth disease and bovine leukosis).

Now at the tender age of 85 years old, I wish to dedicate the remainder of my earthly existence toward the goal of contributing in some way to educating the public in general about the dangers of the adverse effects of alcohol on the brains of adolescents, which can lead to addiction and may ruin their lives and those around them. Wish me luck and success in this endeavor. If you, the reader, have any comments, suggestions, criticisms, or personal anecdotes of interest, please do not hesitate to contact me directly by email at sodendhal505@aol.com,or stewartodendhal@gmail.com In the mean-time enjoy and learn some new things from this book.

Chapter Two
I Stumbled on a New Idea
With My Beautiful Brain

When I first tripped on a high curb in the dark and fell on the concrete side-walk at a motel in Valdosta, Georgia, little did I have any idea that I would become captivated, activated, and obsessed with what the CT technician had told me about the ease with which he could identify alcoholics and drug addicts by how much brain tissue was missing. Figure 1 (also illustrated on the front cover of this book and Figure 2 on the back cover of this book) clearly demonstrates the brain of a chronic alcoholic on the left side compared to an age-related normal non-alcoholic brain on the right side; the missing brain tissue is abundantly obvious at a glance.

My next step was to concentrate on the study of the literature concerning how alcohol can cause the damage that it does to the liver, the gray matter (neurons), and the white matter (supportive glial cells) of the brain. This is taken up in much more detail in chapter four.

Another avenue of investigation involved watching many videos on YouTube having anything to do with alcohol, rehabilitation, or treatment. Then, I read about the federal government and private foundation programs related to substance abuse and statistics on mortality, recovery, case studies, and projections of prevention programs for the future. I also attended Alcoholics Anonymous (AA) meetings on two different continents. I came away with the following conclusion.

Most members of AA that I talked with are not too interested in scientific knowledge about the brain situation and do not really want to bother with learning new ideas. At one of the AA meetings in the city of Prague, Czech Republic, I asked the only woman attendee how old she was when she took her first drink of alcohol. She replied, "I took my first drink when I was 10 years old and it virtually ruined my life. If it had not been for AA, I would not be talking with you right now." J. Griel, who wrote the book, *Never Enough: The Neuroscience and Experience of Addiction,* said that she started drinking alcohol when she was only 13 years old (Griel 2019). Also, in the same book, she made the amazing statement that, *"Each day, ten thousand people around the globe die as a result of substance abuse."* On November 26, 2021, while watching the NBC Nightly News telecast, I heard Kristen Welker (sitting in for Lester Holt) say, *"Every 52 minutes an American die by a drunk driver."* Do we have a problem? Of course, we do!

At an AA meeting in Fort Lauderdale, Florida, when I told an attendee about the technician being able to glance at a CT brain scan and determine if the patient was an alcoholic or drug addict; the person immediately said, "He doesn't know what he is talking about. I'm a nurse and you just can't do that." In actual fact, any lay person can make the same determination, because it is so obvious.

The most impressive experience for me to end my addiction to cigarettes involved the exposure to the comparison between the appearance of normal healthy pink lungs and the black lungs of a smoker; at the medical school in San Francisco, just before I graduated from veterinary school.

After some reflection and thought on the subject of prevention, it seems to me that a new method of educating children, teenagers, college students, and other young adults about the dangers of alcohol should be emphasized and developed. What better way is there, than to show the difference between healthy non-alcoholic's brains and alcoholic brains? If a choice is involved, I don't think that anyone in their rational mind would choose a brain with large vacant spaces in their CT brain scans. Fear is a healthy deterrent from danger and a picture is worth a thousand words or more than thousands of lost neurons. We all are dealt only one brain at birth. It's a shame if we do not take care to keep it in top working order and shape. No wonder many alcoholics make poor decisions when they are utilizing a brain that is missing neurons and has short-circuited white matter connections. It is like playing solitaire with half of a deck of cards instead of a full deck of cards.

My idea is to enlist the assistance of the federal government (the National Institute of Alcohol Abuse and Alcoholism [NIAAA]), private foundations, (e.g., the Hanley Foundation), and state health services (Komro and Toomey 2002) already active in prevention programs for underage drinking. I propose that we start a new strategy to emphasize the danger of brain damage through the involvement of the parents and the communities in sounding the alarm to educate the adolescent population.

As a matter of fact, I was surprised by the lack of emphasis in one publication issued by the NIAAA entitled, '*Alcohol Alert No 72*', where the brain was not mentioned in the text along with the list of organs adversely affected by alcohol. Finding CT brain scans illustrating the missing gray and white matter in long-standing alcoholics was not easy to find, as well as in the current literature. Articles on the information of 'wet brain' or the 'Wernicke-Korsakoff syndrome' which describes the damage to the brain, rarely included CT brain scans; instead, most articles will emphasize that the cause was due primarily to thiamin (vitamin B1) deficiencies. In short, graphic representations of CT brain scans are not easy to find. This should be corrected.

I recall in the early 1950s there used to be advertisements in magazines claiming that there were no dangers from smoking cigarettes, with doctors in white coats illustrating smoking and promoting Chesterfield cigarettes. Years later, in the late 1960s, a warning on every pack of cigarettes carried the statement, *"Caution: Cigarette smoking can be hazardous to your health."* In 2006, a Four Country Survey conducted by the International Tobacco Control evaluating the effectiveness of warning labels to educate smokers was reported (Hammond et al. 2006). This was their main conclusion: *"Smokers are not fully informed about the risk of smoking. Warnings that are graphic, larger, and more comprehensive in content are more effective in communicating the health risks of smoking."*

I suspect that if I were a 7th or 8th grader in junior high school and someone showed me CT brain scans of long-term alcoholics or a drug user's brain, I would be definitely impressed. When I was a teenager back in the mid-1950s in Oklahoma City, Oklahoma, I was well aware of the overdoses of drugs that killed many sports champions and movie stars. I socked away that information and told myself in no uncertain terms if somehow I found myself in a rough crowd that took drugs, I would remove myself from their influence at the earliest possible opportunity. I sincerely believe that if the brain damage by alcohol could be more readily taught and acknowledged among the kids, teachers, parents, and community officials and openly discussed by the entire country, it could be, as they say (whoever they are) 'a game changer'. But of course, this would not be a game changer, per se, because this is not a game, it is a matter of life and death and how some people may live a happy well-adjusted life span or those who die a premature death.

There is already a group of distillers who have formed a foundation that is working and dedicated to the action that kids and alcohol don't mix (Foundation for Advancing Alcohol Responsibility [responsibility.org]). This program called, "Kids and Alcohol Don't Mix" started in 2003 and has reached 140 million parents, teachers, and kids in the grades of 4 to 7. From 2003 to 2016, underage drinking in the study area decreased by 50% (asklistenlearn.org/about/the/development/[Ask, Listen, learn:kids and Alcohal don't Mix]).

Chapter Three
What Motivated Me to Pursue Such an Idea?
(Alcoholics I Have Known)

When I was about 7 or 8 years old, my mother was an attractive, recent divorcee, who worked as an event coordinator and hostess at a private hotel in downtown Oklahoma City, Oklahoma, called the Oklahoma Club. She also had a number of parties at our house and my brother, Charles (who would have been 11 or 12 years old) and I used to stay up late at night at the top of the stairs watching all of the revelers get drunk, wear funny looking hats and stumble around in general, just having fun.

After one of these parties, I went into my mother's bedroom to wake her up because it was after 9:00 in the morning and she still was not yet up and I was getting hungry for breakfast. Her head was completely covered by the pillow and the bed covers looked like a range of mountains. I decided that one of the tallest mountains must have been her shoulder, so I gently shook it. Her head popped out from underneath the pillow and she looked at me. I screamed as loud as I could because I had never seen her or anyone else's face with no eyebrows before.

When she was 14 years old, she saw a movie featuring Marlene Dietrich who had painted eyebrows and she wanted to look just like her. So, she took tweezers and plucked out all of her eyebrows, one hair at a time and they never grew back. When I had calmed down, I said to my mother, "Don't you think that you are just a little bit sober?" (I had confused the term, which I had heard about a lot.)

My mother responded with, "My dear child, 'sober' means, 'not drunk'. And, no, I am not drunk, but I do have a terrible 'hang-over', which is your new word for the day and even though I feel terrible, let's go downstairs and have some bacon and eggs. Shall we?"

Shortly after one of those parties, my mother married the lawyer who handled her divorce from my biological father. And shortly after their marriage, they were divorced because of his alcoholism and he then died, I suspect from esophageal varices rupture.

My mother's third marriage was to another alcoholic, who also was the lawyer that handled her divorce from the first alcoholic. Initially, he was nice to my brother and me, but soon after a short time, he had no desire to pay much attention to us and tended to sort of ignore us. I think he had delusions of becoming our state governor and he ran for district representative to the state legislature, but lost and he began to drink alcohol more than he should. He closed his spiffy law office on the top floor of one of the tallest buildings in downtown Oklahoma City and went to work for a bank. As things were not going his way, he became grouchier, and said repeatedly, "People are no damned good." He and my mother started arguing regularly and playing the blame game with each other.

I remember very distinctly early one morning when he was still drunk staggering around the house; he abruptly just went out the front door of our house and slammed the door shut as hard as he could and started "walking" on the sidewalk, but drifted off periodically and struggled to get back on the sidewalk.

I was worried that he might fall down and so I shadowed his movements by hiding behind the bushes and hedges in the neighbor's front yards. At one point, the sidewalk became a little bit steep heading down the hill. My stepfather struggled to stay on the sidewalk and he went faster than he wanted and he ended up running unintentionally and made a direct hit with his head on a very sturdy tree and fell down.

Because he was inebriated, he was having trouble righting himself to try and stand up. A man watering his flowers in front of his house went running down to help my stepfather stand up. My stepfather yanked the good Samaritan's hand away from his arm and said something like, "Leave me alone, you dumb son-of-a-bitch. I don't need anybody's help." I was so sorry for the neighbor and so sad and embarrassed by my stepfather.

When parties were hosted at our house, at times, after a few drinks under his belt, I saw my stepfather being nasty to some of the guests that were smaller than him. Sometimes, he would try and provoke a fistfight, or physically push someone with whom he was arguing.

My mother must have had enough and she must have told him not to have any more alcohol in the house because

I found a half-pint of Jim Beam half full, hidden in the Oxydol soap box under the kitchen sink when I was doing the dishes one Saturday morning. We decided to adulterate the alcohol in the bottle by adding some of the Oxydol soap flakes as well as some vinegar. After my stepfather got up around 10:00 am, he told everybody that he was going over to the farm he had recently purchased to do some work and he didn't want anyone to go with him. He left the house with a big smile on his face and he was expected back home around supper time. But, he came back in about 30 minutes and wanted to know what we had put into his Jim Beam bottle.

He said that having been raised during the depression when alcoholic beverages sometimes were contaminated and they had to purchase 'Kick-a-poo Indian joy juice', everybody always shook the bottle to see if any foreign substances might be floating around and when he shook his bottle of Jim Beam, all he could see were a bunch of bubbles, so he knew it was contaminated. Somehow he thought the joke we had played had some merit apparently, because he was not angry.

My stepfather went to several different rehabilitation dry-out clinics with very little success, as he always relapsed and would go on a toot as soon as he was released. Finally, my mother had enough; she called the Alcoholics Anonymous (AA) folks and asked for their assistance. They responded by sending over to our house two men, one who had not touched a drop of alcohol for over 7 years and the other gentleman who had been on the 'water wagon' for 14 years and both were much larger than my stepfather.

When they arrived at our house, and walked into the living room. My stepfather recognized that he did not know them, and he bolted for the bedroom and tried to block the bedroom door with a small bookcase. The two men easily push the book case aside and captured my stepfather climbing out of the bedroom window. They explained to my mother that they would take my stepfather out to a restaurant, sit him down, and try and knock some sense into him about his evil ways and they would bring him back in a couple of hours or so. My mother thanked both of them profusely and collapsed onto the living room couch with a sigh of relief.

However, they did not return in a couple of hours. It was close to darkness when the phone rang and they explained that they had found him so entertaining with fantastically interesting stories and telling jokes, that they both decided to just have one drink of bourbon for old-time's sake, which, of course, then led to a couple of drinks more and time got away from them. So, the AA boy's interdiction was a miserable failure.

My stepfather had several drinking buddies and one of them had a wife who just gave up and took their two teenage daughters and moved to Phoenix, Arizona. So, my mother told me to pack my bags and that we were moving to Phoenix because my allergy physician said it would be good for my asthma, but I knew that the real reason for the move was to get away from the chaos and turmoil of living with a dedicated alcoholic.

Because my stepfather's law practice was failing, we had to move from a big house to a little house, but one episode at the big house and its resultant aftermath became a classic story. At the time, I was about 10 years old and my brother, Charles, was about 14 or 15 years old. It was around 9:30 or 10:00 pm on that fateful summer evening that our mother said something like, "Arm yourselves because the evil one is coming back home, even though I told him NOT to come back drunk."

So, Charles and I both chose baseball bats. We went down into the basement and then went up the steps outside slowly to observe the situation when we heard the glass being broken on the door leading into the den on the first floor. What we saw, were two burly police officers holding our stepfather in front of the smashed glass door that our mother had locked. Our mother was leaning out of the bedroom window upstairs pleading for the police to take him away because she was so frightened of him. Our stepfather was saying repeatedly, "I am a (hick) attorney and you cannot (burp) arrest a man, who is tryin' to get into his (hick) own house (hick)."

One of the police officers said, "I'm sorry, lady, but this man is right, we cannot arrest a man for breaking into his own house."

My mother responded, "Please, please, just take him away. I am so frightened, I will not be able to sleep tonight."

Then, my stepfather said, "There, I told you (hick) dumb sons-of-bitches (hick) all along that you cannot (burp) arrest a man breaking into his own house."

To which, one of the police officers said, "Okay, that's it. Slap the cuffs on him, Ralph." Then, facing our stepfather, he continued, "You are being arrested for insulting an officer of the law and we are going to take you downtown and throw you in jail."

About 30 minutes later, the phone rang and my stepfather reported to my mother that at the jail, the night officer was one of his old drinking buddies and he had let him out of jail as soon as the policemen left. My stepfather then said that he was going to the Biltmore Hotel and was going to go to sleep.

The next morning, one of my stepfather's best non-alcoholic friends (who incidentally had an alcoholic wife) was sitting in our living room trying to console my mother when the phone rang. I was in the den right next to the living room. I heard my mother say, "Don't you ever come back here unless you are sober." There was a long pause and I saw my mother put her hand over the speaking part of the phone and she said to my stepfather's non-alcoholic best friend sitting next to her, "He is threatening to jump out of the 25th-floor window of the Biltmore Hotel."

Then, his best non-alcoholic friend said to my mother, "Here, give me that phone." And then he said into the phone, very clearly and slowly, "Do it, do it. Do us and yourself a big favor. Go ahead and jump out of the window from the 25th-floor of the Biltmore Hotel." And then he slammed down the phone into its base.

(The following short stories have been excerpted from my book, *"81 Years of Short Stories: 198 Lessons from My Life for My Grandchildren"*)

1952

FREIGHT YARD WORK

In the summertime, I worked for my uncle at his lumber yard. My cousin, Barney (my uncle's son) also worked there. Our most difficult job was unloading box cars of lumber in the Oklahoma summer heat.

Once we broke the lock on the box car door and opened it; one of us (we alternated) had to crawl up into the very narrow space between the top of the stack of lumber and the top of the boxcar. The lumber was wrapped by an approximately six-inch band of tin to keep the lumber tight and prevent movement which might damage the lumber. We would then take a large heavy tin snip and cut the tin band. However, there was always a problem with getting the orientation of the cutting blades so that they would be at right angles to the tin to effectively cut the tin. If you did not have the blade surfaces at right angles, as the jaws closed, they just slid along the flat surface of the bands and did not cut it. It was actually hard to breathe in the tiny space between the top of the lumber and the top of the boxcar because it was so hot. So, you would have to try for a while and crawl back out of the boxcar to breathe momentarily and then go back in and try again to cut the tin strip.

But I must say, it was one of the best jobs I have ever had. You would work like a dog all day long. And it was strenuous work lifting very heavy stacks of shingles and moving bags of concrete mix, paint cans, etc. But when you got home, blew the black dust out of your nose, and took a long cool shower, you felt great afterward.

A LONG LUNCH HOUR

The junior high school I had attended in Oklahoma City before I went to Phoenix had a sorority called the Happy Hearts. And even though I was now going to Casady high school, one of the prettiest girls in the Happy Hearts invited me as her date to the big sunrise social backward dance that they held once a year. The girls (who were too young to drive) had their mothers drive to the boy's houses and pick them up and take them to the dance which started around midnight (I think). Anyway, we would dance all night long, with breaks for refreshments, and then enjoy a sunrise breakfast. The mothers got the boys back to their houses around 5:30 or 6:00 am.

I was totally exhausted from dancing all night and I knew that if I went to sleep for one hour, I would be incapable of waking up. So, I successfully stayed awake for an hour and then rode my motor scooter to work in the freight yards at 7:00 am.

My uncle, who was the president of the company, had an air-conditioned office with a big Naugahyde couch. The office had one door that opened into the air-conditioned retail show room through which customers and sales people entered and it had another door that opened into the non-air-conditioned back storage area.

My other cousin, Sharon (my uncle's daughter) operated the telephone switch board in the retail show room (a cushy job that made Barney and I green with envy). At lunch time, I was totally exhausted and wanted to rest my weary bones somewhere out of the heat, if possible, to try and recuperate briefly over the lunch hour.

I asked Sharon where her dad was. She said that he had gone to Wichita Falls, Texas on business, and would be gone all day. In a stealthy move, I went into the non-air-conditioned storage area like I was going back to work in the freight yard and carefully opened the door to the president's office, and looked around. Hooray, the air-condition was on and the office was empty. So, I thought that I would just stretch out on the nice Naugahyde couch and rest for just a few minutes before returning back to the freight yards.

The very next thing I remember was that the door to the office opened from the retail side and a strange voice said, "Who's that?"

To which, I heard my uncle say in a matter-of-fact voice, "Oh, that's my no-good lazy nephew." Then, directing his comments to me, he asked, "Stewart, what are you doing here?"

I replied, trying at the same time to brush all of the sawdust and dirt off of his Naugahyde couch, "Oh, I'm just taking a little snooze on my lunch hour."

"Lunch hour?" he exclaimed. "It's 8:00 pm."

To his credit, he didn't fire me, not only because I was his sister's son, but because he probably paid me a lot less than someone else. I explained to him the logistics of the Happy Heart sunrise social backward dance; although he didn't seem to be very sympathetic to that as an excuse for my somnolent behavior.

ESCAPE TO RHODE ISLAND

While my drunken stepfather was beating up a drunken Indian in a motel in Colorado (which horrified my mother), my older brother, Charles, brought up an enticing proposal when I got back home. He asked if I would like to accompany him to go see our real biological father in Rhode Island. I said that was a rhetorical question. Our mother was slated to call us from her "vacation" in Colorado that evening and we could ask her if I could go also.

The phone call followed an anticipated pattern: No, I could not go to Rhode Island because I had asthma and needed to be near doctors. She further explained, "I don't care that you are working in the freight yard. You are frail and you can't go."

Then the great decider came on the phone trying to sound sober. "No, no," my stepfather said. He also said that if I insisted on going, then Charles could not go.

So, we said, "Okay," hung up the phone and then we left for Rhode Island.

DOMESTIC VIOLENCE

One of the reasons I did not relish the idea of returning to Oklahoma City from Rhode Island was because of the shenanigans of my alcoholic stepfather. Little did I realize at the time that I was going from the frying pan into the fire. My stepmother also turned out to be an alcoholic.

My stepmother, Peggy, had been a very successful singer with a British blind piano player named George Shearing, and she was a budding actress in England where she met my father and married him. She was very active in acting in plays in Newport, Rhode Island. One night after the end of one of the plays in which she performed, she got completely drunk at the cast party. Apparently, my dad and she got into some sort of argument. All I remember was some sort of scream that woke me up and very shortly afterward Peggy was standing in the doorway of my bedroom screaming, "See what a wonderful father you have. He just knocked my two front teeth out."

She turned on the light and opened her mouth to show me her missing teeth. There was blood all around her mouth and some dripping off of her chin. After her brief announcement, she turned on her heels and walked into their bedroom. My father came into the room and explained that she was drunk and had threatened to take the girls (my four half-sisters) out into the night and run away. He said, he had no other choice but to hit her when she would not listen to him. His hand was bleeding and portions of the skin from his first interphalangeal joints to the knuckles were missing from two fingers and the bones were exposed.

I asked him if he was all right, did he think that Peggy had settled down, and if would he be okay. He said that he thought everything would be okay and he went into their bedroom and shut the door. No sound came out of the bedroom, so I assumed that everything was okay.

The next morning at breakfast, even with a hangover, they both were discussing the next steps. They both agreed to concoct a story to tell the respective medical authorities about some fictitious accidents that had caused the traumas. My dad said that he would say that he tripped and fell on a porcelain vase and cut his hand. My stepmother said that she would say that she tripped and fell on one of the iron fire place devices and knocked her teeth out.

What amazed me the most, was that both just decided to lie and everything seemed to go back to normal. They were, of course, worried about the consequences of pressing criminal charges with the subsequent investigation and involvement of the police.

My dad wore a bandage around his whole hand for a week or so and Peggy got two new capped teeth from the dentist and that was that.

For Christmas time in 1952, I went back to Oklahoma and moved in with my grandmother who was wonderful and not an alcoholic. My stepfather and mother were divorced and my mother took a job in Dallas, Texas.

One other thought just happened to occur to me about some alcoholics. When I lived in Albuquerque, New Mexico, I had a Certified Public Accountant (CPA) do my income taxes every year I was there. Her office was off of a long hallway that had these fantastic large photographs in black and white displayed along the walls, which were just unusually remarkable and demonstrated a very talented person's insight. When I inquired who was the photographer, the CPA replied, "My cousin, but that is a very tragic story because he was an alcoholic and he committed suicide." Let that thought sink in for a while!

The problem with suicide statistics is that some of them may not have been intentional. For instance, Tiger Woods, a famous golfer, fell asleep while driving his car, ran off the road and almost killed himself. If he had died, there might have been someone who might have claimed that he committed suicide. However, *"A meta-analysis of cohort studies showed that both alcoholics and drug users are strongly associated with suicide. Heavy alcohol consumers had a five-fold higher risk of suicide than social drinkers"* (Pompili et al. 2010).

Chapter Four
The Adverse Effects of Alcohol
on the Brain and
New Discoveries

It is worth reiterating one of J. Griel's opening statements in her book, *Never Enough*: *"Each day, ten thousand people around the globe die as a result of substance abuse"* (Griel 2019).

Ah, the human brain, one of the most exquisite organs of the human body and a master-piece of anatomy and physiology. There is the good news of absolutely astounding new revelations which have recently been discovered of great scientific significance for understanding how the brain works, which we shall examine in some detail later in this chapter. But perhaps at this juncture, the best way to start this chapter is to review the available statistics concerning the use and abuse of alcohol from information provided by reputable official organizations.

The World Health Organization (WHO) estimates worldwide that there are 140 million people suffering from Alcohol Use Disorder (AUD). AUD is the acronym that has been anointed by the psychiatric profession and accepted by other groups studying alcoholism. According to the National Institute of Health (NIH), Alcoholic Use Disorder is, *"A chronic relapsing Brain Disease that causes a person to drink compulsively despite adverse consequences to daily life and overall health"* (Buddy 2020).

The National Institute of Alcohol Abuse and Alcoholism (NIAAA), a subsidiary of the NIH, produced a document entitled, *"Alcohol Facts and Statistics"* in June 2021. This document can be seen on the internet at <niaaa.nih.gov/publications/brochures-and-facts-sheets/alcohol-facts-and-statistics>

These data were collected from a national survey conducted in 2019 concerning the United States only.

Over 14.5 million people in the United States, over 12 years old and older, suffered from AUD in 2019. This included 414,000 teenagers from 12 to 17 years old. Alcohol-related deaths accounted for 95,000 Americans, which included 10,142 deaths by automobile accidents. That number of deaths was 28% of all deadly car accidents. Globally, more than 3 million people died due to Alcohol Use Disorder per year. The economic burden of AUD in the United States for the year 2019 was estimated to be $249 billion.

Other grim statistics from this investigation were disturbing, such as 85.6% of people over the age of 18 years old reported drinking alcohol in their life time, and 25.8% of the people reported binge drinking within the past month. In the report section entitled, *"Alcohol and the human body,"* no mention at all was given about any deleterious effects of alcohol on the brain. Mainly, the damage to the liver was concentrated upon, which disturbed me a great deal, because they ignored the brain destruction. The brain was linked to compulsive drinking in the glossary, however.

In January 2006, the NIAAA released an Alcohol Alert # 67 which dealt with "Underage Drinking." It stated that over 5,000 young people under the age of 21 years old died as a result of underage drinking in the United States: 1,000 via car accidents, 1,600 were from homicides, and 300 were by suicide. Further, the alert claimed that children of alcoholics were more likely to become alcoholics themselves (NIAAA Alcohol Alert # 67, Jan. 2006).

And what about the cost of the treatment of alcoholics? The total spending cost of treating substance abuse in the United States was estimated to exceed $ 21 billion in 2003 and 77% of that amount came from public funds (French et al. 2008). And how successful has the rehabilitation of alcoholics been? *"Despite the advances in science-based for effective preventive interventions and the investments in community-wide preventive interventions, many communities continue to invest in prevention strategies with limited evidence of effectiveness"* (Hawkins et al. 2002). I feel confident that it is fair to say, that the central message of the three previous paragraphs above is: Alcohol abuse can definitely become extremely dangerous to one's health and unnecessarily, extremely costly to society in general. As the former Secretary of Health, Joseph Califano, Jr. said,

"When the use of these substances progresses to the point of meeting medical criteria for abuse or addiction, changes have occurred in the brain which makes cessation of use extraordinarily difficult" (CNN Report 2009).

[The author of this book provided the underlining of the quote above to emphasize the later part of the statement.]

WERNICKE – KORSAKOFF – WET BRAIN

A series of gradual diagnostic changes from Wernicke encephalography to Korsakoff Psychosis to Wernicke-Korsakoff Syndrome (wet Brain) constitute an inevitable slippery slope to oblivion for most fully addicted alcoholics. In order to get an idea of what oblivion looks like for alcoholics, please read Gabor Mate's book entitled, *In the Realm of Hungry Ghosts: Close Encounters with Addiction* (Mate 2010), and the book, *Go Ask Alice* by Anonymous Diary (Anonymous 1999).

Carl Wernicke was a German neurologist, psychiatrist, anatomist, and pathologist who was the first to recognize that the cerebellar cortical degeneration of the brain was associated with chronic alcohol consumption (Wernicke 1881). Wernicke encephalography is characterized by a triad of diagnostic observations: 1. an altered mental state, 2. ataxic gait, and 3. Ophthalmoplegia (a paralysis of the eye muscles) (Vasan and Kumar 2020).

Alcohol blocks the ability of thiamin (vitamin B1) to be absorbed from the gastro-intestinal track (Thomson 2000, Hoyumpa 1980). This leads to a deficiency of thiamin in neurons where vitamin B1 acts as a cofactor for three enzymes needed in carbohydrate metabolism which is necessary to supply energy to the neurons; if vitamin B1 is missing, therefore, it leads to the death of the neurons (Martin et al. 2003). Back in 1982, Harper and Blumberg were the first to demonstrate in a quantitative neuropathological study of brain weights, that the brains of alcoholics actually shrink (Harper and Blumberg 1982). Then in 2009, Harper used Computed Tomography (CT) scans to illustrate the degree of actual shrinkage in the brains of alcoholics (Harper 2009). In a study of 26 heavy drinkers using CT brain scans, 73% (19) showed significant cerebral atrophy (Cala et al. 1978).

The next step in this march toward oblivion is Korsakoff's psychosis. It is possible that sometimes this condition may be referred to as Alcohol-Related-Dementia (ARD) (Ridley et al. 2013). The signs and symptoms of this condition follow: recent memory is adversely affected, learning new skills decrease, mild euphoria, no response to events, personal spontaneity, and incentive decrease, confabulation is often a striking feature, bewildered with unconscious fabrications or confused accounts of events, and they cannot recall even recent previous situations (O'Malley and O'Malley 2020). If you were a parent, would you want to see your offspring go through such psychosis or premature dementia? However, before this stage of psychosis is reached, if an alcoholic abstains from all alcohol ingestion, then, there is a possibility of complete normal brain function to return (Zahr and Pfefferbaum 2017).

The last stage of this march toward oblivion is the Wernicke – Korsakoff Syndrome (wet brain). The signs and symptoms are similar to Korsakoff psychosis, but more severe and prominent. In regards to Wernicke encephalography, there has been only one case study, using Magnetic Resonance Imaging (MRI), where a woman claimed to be a life-long non-alcoholic and was still diagnosed with Wernicke encephalography (Patel et al. 2018). While vitamin B1 deficiency is one of the major causes of neuronal cell death, it was the alcohol that restricted the uptake from the intestinal track, plus the fact that addicts are not known as nutritional fanatics which reduces thiamin intake further. Now that alcohol has been established as indirectly responsible for the death of neurons, is alcohol able to kill neurons directly? The answer is yes. *"Earlier studies have demonstrated that ethanol can cause neuronal cell death through oxidative stress"* (Antonio et al. 2008; Haorah et al. 2008; Heaton et al. 2002, 2003; Lee et al. 2007; Ramachandran et al. 2003; Watts et al. 2005). Recent studies have also indicated increased levels of Reactive Oxygen Species (ROS) in the CNS of alcoholics, probably due to the metabolism of ethanol (Amini et al. 2009). Alcohol is able to cross the Blood-Brain-Barrier and is lipid soluble, so it passes through the vascular endothelial cells easily (Hollville et al. 2019 and [sites.duke.edu.]). Certain proteins (Bax and/or Bak), become activated and insert into the mitochondria outer membrane, a process called, "Mitochondrial Outer Membrane Permeabilization" (MOMP), which causes the release of other proteins which go to the nucleus of the neuron and causes the fragmentation of the DNA that eventually destroys the neuron (Hollville et al. 2019).

But what about the myelin sheaths in the white matter, are they disturbed by exposure to alcohol? Most certainly chronic alcohol exposure can create damage to the myelin pathways throughout the entire brain (Forter 2014). And what kind of damage has been detected? Utilizing the transmission electron microscope, the affected myelin of AUD patients has exhibited irregularly folded lamellae, split lamellae, and some containing vacuoles. It is interesting to note that the myelin in the peripheral nervous system (PNS) is produced by a Schwann cell which wraps the myelin around one single axon; but in the central nervous system (CNS), the Oligodendroglia cells produce myelin around several different axons (Rice and Gu 2019). Now, let's take a look at the good news in the recent scientific discoveries involving fantastic new revelations.

NEUROGENESIS

At the onset, do not let the names of the different parts of the brain disturb you. If you are really interested, you can look up the definitions in the glossary in the appendixes of this book. Just appreciate the thousands of man and woman hours of dedicated scientific investigations, which eventually over-turned the axiomatic statement that human neurons in the brain never divide. From the womb to the tomb, neurons mostly survive until death takes them away at the end of life. No one seemed to ever challenge such a thing.

However, Science magazine published an article in 1992 that shook and electrified the research world of neuroscientists around the globe (Reynolds and Weiss 1992). The authors demonstrated for the very first time that cells from the striatum of the brain of adult mice could be induced to proliferate new neurons *in vitro*, i.e., outside of the body in a laboratory setting. This research killed the dogma that no new neurons could be produced in the central nervous system. This resulted in the christening of a new scientific word called, neurogenesis, which means the generation of new neurons and supportive glial cells.

Six years later, the scientific magazine Nature published an article entitled, *"Neurogenesis in the adult human hippocampus"* (Eriksson et al. 1998). These investigators used *in vitro* methods also, instead of *in vivo*, i.e., within the live animal. With the aid of human cancer patients, they injected Bromodeoxyuridine (BrdU) which becomes incorporated into the DNA of dividing cells undergoing mitosis and can be detected by an immuno-histo-chemical method in their progeny. The controls did not receive any of the BrdU. The Neurogenic Stem Cells (NSC) were generated from the granule neurons in the sub-granular zone of the dentate gyrus of the hippocampus. The NSC are also found in the subventricular zone and are multi-potential precursors of not only neurons but also the cells of the glial supporting elements, such as the astrocytes and oligodendroglial cells. Note that there are 27 different types of neurons in the hippocampus. The investigators also found evidence of NSC (by the BrdU method) in the subventricular zone adjacent to the caudate nucleus (Eriksson et al. 1998).

Two years later, using the technique that Eriksson and his group used to identify NSC (by the BrdU method) discovered that the number of granular cells (NSC) in the dentate gyrus increased in rats who were raised in a stimulating environment, with exercise wheels, mazes, and monkey bars, compared to rats raised in boring cages, over an equal amount of time (Fuchs and Gould 2000). A more recent paper has reported on a functional analysis of the dentate gyrus (Kasner 2018). It should be acknowledged that one of the major functions of the hippocampus is to take, via the white matter, the short-term memories from the prefrontal cortex and send this information to the hippocampus, where it turns the short-term memory into long-term memory and sends it back to the prefrontal cortex (Amthor 2016).

Masaru Tateno and Tashikazu Saito (2008) have found that as alcohol consumption increases, neurogenesis decreases and this leads to atrophy of the brain. Further, they reported upon the 4 stages of neurogenesis: 1. Proliferation, 2. Migration, 3. Differentiation, and 4. Survival. Additionally, with heavy alcohol drinking, the maturation process is apparently blocked some-how during the differentiation stage. In a complex cascade of events, alcohol activates a transcription factor (cAMP – response element protein [CREB]), which targets certain genes in the nucleus to turn on and increase the survival of the neuron – alcohol decreases this system requirement for the survival of the neuron. The hippocampus atrophy occurs in alcoholism, and the cessation of alcohol consumption then allows the repopulation of the brain from the NSC that fill out the spaces of the brain (Tateno and Saito 2008).

GLYMPHATIC

For decades neuroscientists wondered why there were no lymphatics in the parenchyma of the Central Nervous System (CNS) of the brain. However, there was one strange fact that bothered some people: in the peripheral nervous system (PNS), most of the larger arteries and veins tend to run in close association with nerves and each other throughout the PNS, while in the CNS, the larger arteries and veins are separated by some distance from each other.

A neuroscientist in Denmark by the name of Majken Nedergaard discovered the reason for the different vascular patterns between the PNS and the CNS. Her articles in eclectic science journals were proclaimed the most important research publications for the whole year of 2015 (Nedergaard 2015). There is a collapsible and expandable rarely observed space surrounding the larger arteries in the brain called, "peri-arteriolar space," which becomes filled with cerebral spinal fluid (CSF) during a segment of night time sleep and when mammals are anesthetized. The peri-arteriolar space is completely collapsed in histologically prepared slides, and that accounts for the reason that the expanded peri-arteriolar space around these arteries had never been noticed before in the brain.

So, what is the big deal about this space and why was it considered such a significant discovery? Well, first of all, it is all about what happens to the bulging and pulsating CSF in the peri-arteriolar space which has an outer wall or membrane, that on the other side of which thousands of astrocytes cover this membrane with specially designed foot-plates. These foot-plates have what are called "water channels" or little tiny potential holes in the cellular membrane (Badaut et al. 2002). These holes are formed by a protein called Aquaporin-4 (or AQP-4) which must be sensitive to pressure or some other trigger, to change their shape, such as to form the "water channel," which is a marvel of dimensional architecture, as it forms a channel just large enough to allow individual H20 molecules (2.6 angstroms wide) to pass through into the astrocyte cell body. (Please be aware that there are, 100,000,000 angstroms in one centimeter.) But then on the other side of the astrocyte cell body is a large number of "potential water channels" which allows the water to flood the extracellular spaces in order to flush out all of the debris and cellular metabolic waste around the neurons and glial elements toward the peri-venous space next to a vein passing through modified astrocytes to reach the blood and exit the brain; eventually going to the cervical lymph nodes via true lymphatics passing through the foramen magnum (Jessen, et al. 2015, Benveniste et al. 2019). In essence, the Glymphatic system acts as a night-time custodian sweeping up all of the trash from daily activities to keep the brain clean and operating correctly. The bulk of glymphatic cleaning takes place during the deep sleep phase when the slow wave activity is most abundant (Faust 2019). The "G" in the word, Glymphatic is from the Greek word "glia," meaning glue which refers to all of the glial cells supporting neurons, such as astrocytes, oligodendroglial cells, and microglial cells.

I apologize if I told the reader more about this system than they may have wanted, but the whole system is absolutely fascinating to me. I did not even tell the reader about the fact that it has been reported that this tiny water channel that allows space for only one molecule of water to pass through at a time, can allow a total of one million molecules of water to pass through in one single second (Nagelhus and Ottersen 2013). The multipotential astrocytes constitute the largest cell population in the brain and support neurons and other glial elements in many ways. There are eleven different aquaporin proteins in the human body, named by numbers one through ten and one named zero (Nagelhus and Ottersen 2013). The first aquaporin was discovered in red blood cells (Benga 2015). The location and relevance of all eleven aquaporin proteins have been described (Takata 2004).

What in the future does the glymphatic system offer as a possible benefit to the general public? As an example, when the glymphatic system is flushing out all the accumulated trash, the glial cells shrink their size significantly in order to not impede the free flow of the water to the venous side of the area to be cleaned. MRI studies have shown that in Alzheimer's Disease, the glial cells do not shrink at night, therefore, the debris is not removed easily. So, there are researchers looking to see how to get the glial cells to behave appropriately and shrink (Nedergaard 2015). I would encourage everyone to go online to YouTube and see Nedergaard's video of her Stanford University presentation on glymphatic and her cooperative research efforts with world experts in other ancillary fields of inquiry. In the search space on YouTube, just type, "Nedergaard; Glymphatic" and there you go. She mentions in this presentation that she and other investigators have also confirmed that if one sleeps laterally, with the right side of one's head on the pillow, that is the most helpful in removing beta-amyloid and tau proteins during the cleaning cycle (Nedergaard YouTube, Glymphatic; Stony Brook University 2015).

HOW AND WHY DO THE GLIAL CELLS SHRINK AT NIGHT

If the astrocytes and oligodendroglial cells (the main glial cells) did not shrink up to 60% of their size (Walker

2017), the efficiency of the trash flushing operation would undoubtedly be less successful in their cleaning responsibilities. In this opened-up space between the glial elements, certain proteinaceous materials accumulate and may form large aggregates of protein globs that present a problem in gaining access across the astrocyte foot plates in order to reach the peri-venous space. The astrocytes' foot-plates on the peri-venous space, must have gaps between them to allow the efflux of larger entities that obviously cannot travel through the water channels of the AQP-4 membrane proteins. Two notorious proteins that present such a problem are beta-amyloid and Tau, both of which play a dominate role in brain diseases like Alzheimer's and Parkinson diseases. This narrative explains why the glial shrinkage is important, but not "how" it is triggered. The evidence so far, strongly suggests that norepinephrine which is both a hormone and a neurotransmitter is released from the locus coeruleus in the small area of the pons and may be the stimulus that opens up the water channels and begins the custodial activity (O'Donnell et al. 2015). As one can see, more research is needed to expand on the fantastic work that has been accomplished so far.

Chapter Five
How I Quit Smoking for Good
After a 15-Year Addiction

"It is notoriously hard to quit smoking, a combination of habits being hard to change and nicotine's particular form of withdrawal" (Griel 2019). I can easily attest to that statement. But, perhaps it might be more instructive if I analyze how I got started on the evil weed in the first place and go from there.

I never had a desire to smoke cigarettes or marijuana, but when most of my buddies that I hung around with in high school were all smoking, I decided to try it out. I thought if I did not like it, I could quit easily. But I decided that it looked cool and I felt like I appeared more mature. Also, in those early days of the 1950s, very little medical dangers of smoking were in the public press at that time. So, I just coasted along with the crowd.

(The following anecdote is excerpted from my book, *81 Years of Short Stories: 198 Lessons from My Life for My Grandchildren*).

DON'T EVER LIE TO YOUR GRANDMOTHER

In desperation, my mother divorced my alcoholic stepfather and left town. She went to Dallas, Texas and I went to live with my grandmother in Oklahoma City. All of my cousins and my brother called her mama Stewart, but I just called her mama, because that's what my mother called her and I always called her the same name.

Like most of my pals, I started smoking cigarettes when I was in the 10th grade. After living with my grandmother for about a year and a half, she posed a question to me. She said, "Stewart, you're not smoking cigarettes are you?"

"Nope, Mama," I replied casually lying.

A few weeks went by and again Mama asked me the same question and I gave her the same answer.

Another few weeks went by and again she asked me if I was smoking, as she had seen a number of young kids my age smoking.

At this constant questioning, I became angry. "Gosh darn it, Mama, you keep asking me the same question and I am getting tired of it. Do you think that I would lie to my own grandmother that I love so very much? Quit bugging me about it and leave me alone."

Mama was quiet for a minute. The silence bothered me and I thought, maybe I was too severe with her and she could not take the shock of me barking back at her. Then she said, "You know, Stewart, you will be going away to college one of these days and perhaps it might be important to you to be able to wash your own white shirts."

Now I thought, *She's flipped out and she doesn't even know what she's doing.* I decided to humor her and do as she suggested when she asked me to follow her into the kitchen.

On the kitchen counter were my white shirts, underwear, T-shirts, socks, etc. Patiently standing behind her trying to conceal my boredom, my mama said, "Notice that the first thing you do, is to empty all of the loose tobacco out of the shirt pockets."

Stunned at this unexpected revelation, I stammered, "Oh, Mama, I have been carrying Bernie Hodge's cigarettes around for him because he doesn't want his mother to know that he is smoking."

She just looked at me straight in my eyes and sympathetically stated the coup de grace, "Stewart, you have been carrying around Bernie Hodge's cigarettes since before he even moved to Oklahoma City."

"Uh, oh. You got me, Mama. You are absolutely right. I apologize. I have been lying to you and I am sorry. I will never lie to you again. I promise." And thus ended the first lesson.

After several years, I did decide to try and stop smoking on my own. I was motivated because I realized that I was truly addicted. This inconvenient fact dawned upon me one time when I wanted to smoke so badly that I could not wait for the movie I was attending to get over, that I missed the end of the movie and I went into the men's room, sat on the toilet seat and smoked a cigarette. I remember thinking at the time, *My god, Odendhal, you are so addicted to smoking, that you can't even control your own brain and you let this bloody habit control you.*

So, I made a weak attempt to stop smoking, failing measurably with every embarrassing plan I could dream up.

Once, I threw half of a pack of unsmoked cigarettes out the window of the car as I was driving down the street. Another time, I told myself to chain-smoke one whole pack of cigarettes to become disgusted with myself. Unbelievably, after only the second straight cigarette, I felt ill and had to stop right then and there.

Then there was the time that I gave half of a carton of cigarettes to a prisoner of a chain-gang working on a road in Alabama when I was a student at the University of the South.

Then, when I was studying at the University of California at Los Angeles (UCLA) some of my friends were always bumming Lucky Strike cigarettes from me. On a trip to Tijuana on the Mexican border, I bought a couple of packs of Delicados cigarettes. They were terrible, the tobacco was filled with various sizes of shreds of tobacco, and some of them looked almost like miniature stumps, which smelled and tasted bad. But these cigarettes provided a method whereby, I discouraged the cigarette bummers to stop asking me for a cigarette. Because the Delicados pack was slim, I would put the pack in front of my Lucky Strikes in my shirt pocket and when someone would ask if they could bum a cigarette, I would remove the Delicados pack and offer them to take one out of the pack. They never asked me again.

As a first-year veterinary student, we studied the anatomy and histology of the lungs, and I began to think that it might not be a bad idea if I stopped smoking. From previous experience, I knew that it would be a hard battle, so I bought a book with the title of (wait for it!), *How to*

Stop Smoking, and it was truly a clever and useful book. I still remember the strategy and logic presented.

The very first thing to do is to figure out a date to start the project, preferably about a month away, when you were sure that you will have a prospective calm atmosphere to operate in with no stress. Once you have selected the date, literally tell all of your friends that you are going to quit smoking on that date and within two weeks you were going to succeed. And tell your friends to tell their friends to tell them about your plans and your commitment to see this project to the end. I had worked before veterinary school for two years for a pharmaceutical manufacturing company and they had agreed to hire me back for the summer vacation.

The very next thing that one does, is to write down all of the reasons that you are going to quit smoking. In my case, it was a very long list: 1. It was not a healthy thing to do, 2. The cigarettes burned a hole in my best cashmere sweater, 3. I dropped my lit cigarette between my legs as I was driving my car on a very busy road and had a hell of a time finding it before pulling off of the road, 4. I hated scrapping off the yellow coat of nicotine off of the inside of the front wind-shield window, 5. Girls did not like my breath, 6. It was expensive at 19 cents a pack, 7. Having to empty the ash tray and get the ashes to scatter all over the car interior, 8. How to put the cigarette out at the end while driving. I think I ended up with about 27 reasons why I wanted to quit smoking. Then every day for a week, I was supposed to congratulate myself on these reasons for quitting and have my brain convince me that this is the best plan and I will succeed for sure. By repeating this daily, you sort of brain washed yourself into believing that you will do it for sure.

On the appointed day, I told everyone this was the start date, and I intended to succeed, and, of course, my friends all laughed at me, which made me more committed and led me to tell myself, *I'll show you jerks that I am going to do it.*

The first few days were the worse. On the second or third day, I was just dying for a cigarette. The book had told me that it is good to have something to do with your mouth when the going got rough, like sucking on a tooth pick, chewing on chewing gum, buying some life savers, or letting your tongue play with a safety pen or a paper clip in your mouth. I selected life savers. The next day, I felt very painful canker sores all over the mucous membranes inside of my mouth and also all over my tongue. It was very difficult to talk, eat or move my tongue anywhere. This lasted for at least two more days and then slowly (too slowly for me), it just disappeared (thank God). I succeeded in not smoking at all, all summer long.

When veterinary school started for my second year I did not smoke the first week. Then something I had not prepared for occurred. The second week of school and I was studying for a test that I was to have the following day. Trying to memorize some of the more difficult material, I kept being distracted from studying and a little devil in my brain kept repeating, *If you had a cigarette, perhaps you could concentrate better on the test material and be better prepared for the test.* Before, I knew it, I ran down to the drug store and bought a pack of Lucky Strikes and was puffing away until the next summer vacation was just around the corner between my second and third year of veterinary school.

This time, I had been hired to join a research project on seals and sea lions operated by the Stanford Research Institute and it was going to be exciting, stimulating, and just plain fun. So, I knew that I could quit smoking again for the summer. And, following the same game plan, I was successful. However, on the second or third day, I wanted a cigarette very strongly and I was thinking about going to buy a pack of cigarettes or life savers, but I remembered that the summer before, the life savers had caused these horrible canker sores (I thought). I must have been wrong blaming the lifesavers because I was getting the same damned canker sores again without the lifesaver this time.

A very interesting change in my attitude developed in the very early stages of not smoking. During school and during the non-smoking summer, I would get up early and run a mile along the railroad track, turn around, and run back to the trailer park where I lived. I thought that my time running should have improved when I quit smoking, but it didn't. The timing of the run stayed the same. I was not disappointed that I could not run any faster; I was elated that I did not have a craving for cigarettes anymore and felt like I was no longer addicted to something that controlled me and I was free to make my own choices and decisions from now on. It was a great feeling of freedom.

I guess it must have been predictable and I should not have been surprised, but the night before my first test and the stress, I bought a pack of cigarettes and started smoking once again as I entered into my third year of veterinary school.

For my third summer vacation, I was hired by a veterinarian employed by the U.S. fish and wildlife Service to perform necropsies on dead fur seal pups on the Pribilof Islands in the middle of the Bering Sea next to Alaska. The word necropsies mean necro = dead and opsies = to look at; it is similar to autopsies in human medicine which means auto = self and opsies = to look at.

As soon as I finished my third year of veterinary school, I drove to Seattle and did some camping and sight-seeing around Seattle (beautiful area). Unfortunately, my veterinarian boss insisted that I quit smoking and I should have done it. But my foolish pride just would not allow him to dictate how I should live my life and I just refused to give into his demands. So, I continued to smoke cigarettes all summer and throughout my last year in vet school.

Now we approach the real reason why I stopped smoking for good and that requires a preamble. There was a custom that during the last month of our senior year of study, the senior students of the veterinary school would spend one day at the medical school in San Francisco and the next week, the senior students at the medical school would spend one day at the veterinary school. This exchange was very popular and it was called simply "Senior Med Day."

During the visit to the medical school, we learned many things, such as the medical students did not refer to their rotation through pediatrics, as pediatrics, they would ask each other, for example, "When are you going to rotate through veterinary medicine (since babies could not talk and sometimes acted like animals)." But two presentations at the medical school were especially of interest to me; i.e., psychiatry and pathology. In those days of the year 1967, the hippy community of San Francisco was located in the Hate Ashbury district, which began just a block or so next to the medical school.

The psychiatrist started his presentation by explaining that he wanted to begin some research on LSD (Lysergic Acid Diethylamide), but no federal agencies would fund any research efforts on an illegal drug. So, he would have to fund his own support. As luck would have it, one day he walked over to a drugstore in the Hate Ashbury district to buy some cigarettes. When he went to pay for the cigarettes at the cashier's counter he noticed a placard with a method of how to produce LSD. He hastily copied down the information and changed his teaching schedule to include a plan to engage the senior class for a quick research program featuring LSD.

The next day during his lecture to the class of students, he told them that he was going to do some experiments with LSD and wanted their participation. It would be completely voluntary and they would have to sign a document that they were not coerced in any way. He then explained the project. About half of the class agreed to participate. The plan was that half of those participating would receive either a cup of LSD and the other half of participants would receive a placebo in a similar-looking cup, i.e., no LSD. Then he asked everybody to write down what they would expect to experience if they received the LSD and hand that to him for safe keeping.

The next day of his class, he asked that all non-participants to leave the lecture hall and he would distribute the LSD or the placebo to the participants. At the end of the hour, each student should write what they actually felt following their consumption of the material in the cup they were handed.

First of all, none of the students had received LSD; all of the students had received a placebo. When the professor read the expected experience and the actual experience, almost all of them were almost the same which he found amazing and unexpected on his part. For example, if a student had expected to see pink elephants marching upside down on the ceiling before the experiment, they would report the same situation after drinking the false "LSD" liquid. I don't think that the psychiatrist ever sent the study in for publication somewhere, but the results were still very interesting anyway.

Now we come to the pathology department display. In a large room, there were distributed organ samples from recent autopsy examinations. The one that was most disturbing to me was the comparison of a smoker's lung compared to a non-smoker's lung. The non-smoker's lung was pink and had a very smooth surface, while the smoker's lung was black and did not have a smooth surface. It was a dramatic example which most probably would have a lasting impact on any smoker. Somehow, I want to publicize the contrast between the damaged brains of unbeautiful substance abuse addicts and the normal intact beautiful brains and scare the hell out of kids, adolescents, and teenagers for their own good and that of society in general.

I did have one relapse to start smoking again once in India for only one day because of a totally unexpected incident of great stress which is outlined in the following anecdote.

(This story is excerpted from my book entitled, *"1968 – My First Year in India with Johns Hopkins: Tales of Indo-U.S. Mutual Cross-Cultural Enlightenment"*)

I LOST THE WILHELM'S SUITCASES

(The Wilhelms were a couple that my wife, Bobbie, and I met in New Delhi at a three-week orientation meeting for American scientists who were new to India. Don was conducting research in the state of Uttar Pradesh and his wife, Alana had invited her niece and nephew, Leal and Brian, over from the U.S. to learn about India from a short visit to Calcutta to see us).

On the 17th of September, 1968, it was a bright and shiny morning that did not foretell the catastrophic events about to unfold in our mutual destiny. I had hired two men with rickshaws to take Wilhelm's luggage to the Singur Railway Station and with great effort we all got on the train to Howrah at the last minute. The ride to Howrah Train Station was uneventful (something unusual). At the Howrah Train Station, we got in the line for taxis and slowly progressed toward the end of the line controlled by policemen, who assigned the customers to the various taxis nearby. That was the point of departure from normality to calamity.

The taxi driver would not let all of us into the same taxi. After our ruptured Bengali and all of the confusion and gesticulations, it dawned upon us that all of the luggage would not fit into one trunk, so, Bobbie rode with Don and Alana, and Leal, and Brian, rode with me in another taxi; with the suitcases equally distributed into the trunks of the two taxis. Off we went to reconnect at the Fairlawn Hotel in Calcutta.

The traffic as usual was horrible and our respective taxis were soon separated. I arrive at the Fairlawn Hotel first. The Fairlawn Hotel had a very short driveway, just wide enough for two taxis to stop side by side next to the opened area where the reception desk was located. There was no way for a vehicle to turn around; they had to back into the street, which was only a car length from where the taxis had to stop to unload.

As we pulled into the empty parking area and the taxi stopped. I looked over to the reception desk and saw a very shapely figure of a white Caucasian female in a beautiful blue sari, with long brunette hair, a bare mid-drift, a slim waist, and a perfect-looking derriere. I could not contain myself, as a flood of testosterone must have propelled my brain to force me to immediately pay the taxi driver and I hopped out of the taxi in a mad desire to see if the lady's face was as beautiful as the rest of her.

As I raced toward the desk, unfortunately, the object of my fascination disappeared up the stairs and out of sight. As I turn around, I saw Brian and Leal standing next to me, but the taxi was backing quickly out of the driveway into the street and out of my sight. Nonplussed, I then asked the clerk if they had accommodation for the Wilhelm family and he answered in the affirmative. Pleased with his response and still savoring the reemergence of the image of the lady in the blue sari, I saw the other taxi pull into the parking area.

As Bobbie and the Wilhelms exited their taxi and were gathering up their personal items and took their luggage out of the trunk, I said, "I've good news. They have room for you all here tonight."

Don, looking around, nonchalantly, asked, "Where are the other suitcases?"

Slapping my right hand against my forehead, I shouted, "The suitcases! Oh, my God, I forgot about them. I left them in the taxi and he just drove away."

Don looked at me in disbelief and after a short pause he said, "Come on, Odendhal, surely you gest."

I stammered, "Believe me. I'd give anything to say that I am just kidding, but I can't. I am so sorry. This is a disaster." I stood there disgusted with myself.

Don became frantic when he realized that I was not having fun, but was, indeed, telling the truth. He ran in one direction a short distance, turned, and then ran in another short distance, back and forth, saying, "We've got to do something. All of our clothes, passports, airline tickets, and over 3,000 rupees were in those suitcases."

I ran to the reception desk and asked where was the owner, Mrs. Smith. The receptionist said that she was just now coming down the stairs. I ran up to the landing and said, "Mrs. Smith, the taxi that I was in, just drove off with all of my friend's luggage and—"

Before I could finish my sentence, she looked at me with disbelief and said, "Why did you do something so stupid?"

"For Christ's sake, I didn't do it on purpose," I responded.

"Don't take the name of the Lord in vain in my hotel," she hollered back.

"I'm sorry, but what do you think we should do?"

"Well, call the police, the taxi associations, the newspapers, and the consulate. Hell, call everybody, and put your brain back together."

Leaving out her last statement, I ran back down the stairs and related most of what Mrs. Smith had told me. After a brief discussion, we divided up our respective duties. I would go back to the Howrah Train Station and attempt to recognize the same taxi driver as the taxis funneled through the taxi line; hoping that the driver was innocent of premeditated theft and had unintentionally driven out with the suitcases. Don and Brian would go to all of the taxi associations and newspapers, Alana and Leal would go to the American consulate, and airline ticket offices. Bobbie would go to the Higashi's and Schad's (other American Hopkins scientists in Calcutta) seeking clean clothes for them. We all agreed to reassemble around 5 pm, back at the hotel.

Completely discouraged and mad at my testosterone, I took a taxi back to Howrah Station and began my vigilant search for the errant taxi driver. I stood most of the time slightly off of the end of the taxi line where I could get a good look at the drivers as they pulled out of the taxi stand. They drove by non-stop, but I never saw one that came close to the driver we had.

About halfway through the day, thinking of how I was going to pay for all of the rupees and cover their other losses, I became very depressed. I could not help myself, I started smoking cigarettes again (another dumb thing to do).

Bobbie and Alana picked me up in a taxi and we went back to the Fairlawn Hotel. The ground floor of the hotel was in the shape of a large "U." The inside of the "U" was the dining hall, with rooms surrounding it. The dining area opened onto a lounge area with tables and chairs where beer was served in front of the reception desk. Then, there was a garden all the way to the wall separating the property from the street. We congregated in the lounge.

Each of us related our experiences and we discussed our next move. We had dinner and reassembled back in the lounge. Suddenly, a small, very thin man dressed in an ill-fitting suit walked up to our table and said, "Excusing you, would any here be Mr. Wilhelm just now?"

Don responded, "Yes. I am Mr. Wilhelm. What can I do for you?"

With a flamboyant air, the man said, "The more important affair, is what can I do for you? I am Inspector Bhattacharjee with the Calcutta secret police and I have good news. I am confident that we shall catch the evil taxi driver, as my agents are all over town and we have infiltrated all organizations of every kind all over Calcutta. You see, it is just a matter of time before we snatch the deranged perpetrator of this crime."

With this apparently memorized preliminary introduction completed, he sat down in an empty seat beside us and lit a cigarette.

All of us were somewhat taken aback and each of us glanced back and forth to see each other's reactions. I don't remember if any of us asked to see his identification, but he was very entertaining. He then launched into his background and explained that he had been a refugee during the partition of British India from East Pakistan (now Bangladesh). He hated his job. He hated Calcutta and only dreamed of returning to East Pakistan.

Don said, "If you hate it here so much, why don't you go back then?"

"Why?" he said followed by a short pause. "For the simple reason that the Muslims will kill me."

Don then asked, "How can you be so sure that you will catch the evil party?"

"You see, with our spies infiltrated into all of the organizations of Calcutta, one of them is sure to vomit to me the information who done it."

As he talked, he had a habit of dramatically periodically flicking his cigarette ashes onto the floor, ignoring the ashtray right next to him. He was a good source of comic relief. He left the premises at about 9:00 pm. The Wilhelms went to bed and Bobbie and I took the 10:40 pm train back to Singur.

When we got back to our house around midnight, we saw where robbers had tried to get into our house. The next morning, I had to wait around for Gour, the field station carpenter, who could fix the broken window so Bobbie and I could go back to Calcutta by train. I was very depressed and completely down.

When we arrived at the Fairlawn Hotel, we learned that the suitcases had been returned with everything in them untouched and nothing was missing. Jubilation reigned in the lounge. All of our (not my) legwork had paid off. The front page of the English language newspaper had the story of the presumed thief captioned, "Another American couple duped by a taxi driver." Because all of the taxi associations had been contacted, when the taxi driver eventually discovered the suitcases, he knew where to return them.

After the taxi left the Fairlawn Hotel, the driver did not have a reason to open the trunk until very late the same day. Then, when he did open the trunk at Howrah Station, the other drivers told him about the situation and he drove back to the Fairlawn and gave them to the Wilhelms the next morning.

During all of the elation, I toyed with the idea that I would tell the Wilhelms that I had planned the whole thing to provide them with some excitement and entertainment. But, finally using my brain for the first time in days, I dropped that idea like a hot potato.

My relapse back to smoking cigarettes, lasted only one day. The cigarettes are called *bedis*. They are small, do not last long, and have an irritating smell (sort of reminded me of Mexican Delicados), so I only smoked one of them and did not buy any more.

Chapter Six
An Improved Educational Public Health Program for Would Be Alcoholics

There is a serious problem concerning how children, adolescents, teenagers, and young adults are educated about how the dangers of alcohol are introduced to them, i.e., they are ineffective and incomplete in most cases. For some unknown reasons, even the top federal agencies are reluctant to reveal the truth of the extent of brain damage in those suffering from AUD. For example, the National Institute of Alcohol Abuse and Alcoholism, in their *"Alcohol Facts and Statistics"* section of *"Alcohol and the Human Body,"* made no mention of the damage to the brain. Instead, most of the report was about the liver (NIAAA Alcohol Facts and Statistics, June 2021). The Center for Disease Control and Prevention (CDC.gov/alcohol/fact-sheet/prevention.htm) did not mention about brain damage at all.

I am not big on clichés, but I like the one that says, *"An ounce of prevention, is worth a pound of cure."*

Just a few minutes ago on Christmas day, 2021, I read an article that I received in my email from Medscape Medical News, which is circulated online for medical professionals. The title of the article was, *"Moderate Alcohol's Health Benefits Look Increasingly Doubtful."* The author pointed out that, the *"Current established guidelines"* say *"that a little bit of alcohol now and then actually has robust health benefits."* He goes on to say, *"Emerging data calls into question whether alcohol in moderation should really continue to be just what the doctor ordered."*

Under a sub-heading of the article, i.e., *"Alcohol's Diminishing Cardioprotective Value,"* the author states, *"The benefits of light to moderate alcohol consumption – usually defined as 1 to 2 drinks a day – has been its proposed cardioprotective value."* This supposition is being challenged lately by several reputable resources.

Under another sub-heading (An Overlooked Carcinogen), the author states, *"Surveys indicate that less than half of Americans realize alcohol increases as a cancer risk."* Another author finished the last sentence of his article by saying, *"There is no safe limit of alcohol consumption."* And, the American Cancer Society, which updated its guidelines in 2020 after an 8 years hiatus, said, *"It is best not to drink alcohol."* The Medscape article ended with, *"But we have to stop presenting that it (alcohol) is good for us because it isn't."* (Watson 2021).

I apologize for this last-minute diversion, but it is important when dangerous medical advice is being challenged and adjusted. And now back to our regularly scheduled topic of improving the public health message of the dangers of alcohol to those who are most vulnerable.

In order to formulate an improved and more realistic and successful public message for the education of adolescents against alcohol use, I will briefly just recapitulate my personal experiences leading toward that goal.

Step 1. I was informed that I had a beautiful brain compared to alcoholics and drug users.

Step 2. I confirmed (beyond a reasonable doubt) that the above statement was true, by investigating the literature and CT brain scans published in reputable journals.

Step 3. The people I met at AA meetings did not seem particularly interested in hearing about brain damage caused by alcohol, or scientific studies to understand the nature of the damage.

Step 4. Rehabilitation and preventive programs, both appear to be ineffective in both the recovery of alcoholics and protecting adolescents from initial consumption of alcohol.

Step 5. There has to be a better way to inform and educate the general public about the oblivion that AUD sufferers face, or the general public remains ignorant of the consequences of addiction.

Step 6. A graphic and dramatic campaign should be instigated to illustrate the grotesque nature of alcoholic brains for shock value as a deterrent.

Step 7. My present intention is to contact, in the next few months, most of the foundations, federal government agencies, and non-government organizations (NGOs) dedicated to educating the public citizens about the damaged brains of those addicted to alcohol and seek financial support to standardize such a strategy. The greater the number of people who know about this problem, the greater the prospects there will be to help the people who suffer with AUD and help prevent young people from being enticed to drink alcohol in the first place.

Chapter six illustrates how sometimes common medical statements may not always have the most appropriate veracity and should be met with some reservation. Also, emphasis on public health posture regarding AUD may not have an eye-catching attraction and may need to address a more effective theme to educate the general target population. I was advised by physicians to take Vioxx, a Cox-2 inhibitor on a daily basis to treat arthritis, and the next thing I knew, the Vioxx was recalled by the FDA (Food and Drug Administration) because of the side effect of heart attack and strokes. But by that time, I had already had my double bypass operation to correct major clots in two main cardiac arteries.

Then later, another physician convinced me to agree to take statin medication daily to prevent clots, but after months of horrendous muscle pain, I stopped taking statins and my muscle pain disappeared completely. Now, because of atrial fibrillations, I have been taking Eliquis daily, which is an anti-coagulant and I could not stop taking the Eliquis if I wanted to, because possible clots would form throughout my body. So, the BREAKING NEWS presented in this chapter is like music to my ears. I strongly suspect that the damage to the brain in substance abuse patients is downplayed and should be known by all who drink alcohol, or take drugs and the truth expanded to the whole world.

Chapter Seven
At the End of the Trail

In this next to the final chapter, I want to emphasize and describe what are some of the long-term consequences of the initial swallow of alcohol and the horrible trail that follows which may end in tragedy. Unfortunately, not only does this tragedy affect the alcoholic; it is a tragedy that tears at the very fiber of the whole family of survivors, but also all humans with whom the alcoholic may have come into contact.

Around 10:30 pm in my home in Georgia, I received a telephone call from a stranger I had never heard of before from Chico, California. She was a neighbor of Chrissy, my youngest half-sister. The lady (whose name escapes me) explained to me that I and my other half-sisters had to do something about Chrissy's drinking, as Chrissy was jeopardizing her marriage with her own husband because she was spending so much time looking after Chrissy and her drinking problem.

On this latest occasion, she described that Chrissy had passed out on the living room floor and was lying in her own filth with several empty bottles of vodka scattered on the floor. The lady asked that me and my other siblings should pay for Chrissy to be institutionalized at a rehabilitation establishment where they could take care of her.

The lady added that after she had been successful in reviving Chrissy slightly, she said to her still lying on the floor, "Don't you know that drinking so much alcohol can kill you? Do you really want to kill yourself?"

To her complete surprise, Chrissy answered, "Perhaps that might not be such a bad idea."

I was mortified to learn of her statement which seemed so pitiful to me and such a bad sign. I explained to the lady that we had enrolled Chrissy in several dry-out programs, but she always just walked out on her own after about a week or so. It was only about two or three weeks after that telephone call that Chrissy's son, Phil, called to tell me that Chrissy had passed away. Just another premature death due to alcohol which robbed herself and our family of her delightful personality.

Before I get into the statistics of how alcohol and drugs cheat people of many potential years of their lives, I feel the need to share a recent anecdote of another disturbing nature involving teenage overdosing.

In mid-February of 2022, I was invited to attend a town hall meeting to learn about and discuss the alcohol and drug problems in the community of Pompano Beach, Florida. One of the members of the panel, who was either a police officer or a social worker had the job of interviewing the family members and writing a report for the city government. What he said was shocking to me, he said that since January first that 12 to 17 teenagers had died of drug overdosing. That is more than one death per week which seems way too many.

He continued that the drug dealers were lacing drugs like heroin, cocaine, and methamphetamine with fentanyl which makes those drugs much stronger and accounts for the larger number of deaths.

Later on, he choked up and took his handkerchief out to wipe away his tears and confessed that he hated his job because it was so painful to observe families talking about their suffering and loss, that he wanted to quit his job. So, the actions of alcoholics and drug users can bring depression and despair to those they don't even know.

Most people who take their first drink of alcohol seem to do that at a friend's house; just read, *"Go Ask Alice"* (Anonymous 1999), *"Never Enough"* (Griel 2019), and *"The Teenage Brain"* (Jensen 2015), whether it was of their own volition, or surreptitiously. Once on the trail of alcoholism, that slipper slope may have tragic consequences, such as premature death.

The CDC Morbidity Mortality Weekly Report published a paper by (Esser et al. 2020) entitled, *"Death and Years of Potential Life Lost from Excessive Alcohol Use – United States 2011–2015. Weekly/October 2, 2020, 69(39); 1428–1433."* This report established that excessive alcoholic consumption when linked with 58 different human diseases can cause death to the individual involved. This observation is listed as Alcohol-Related Disease Impacts (ARDI). An ancillary observation is listed as Years of Potential Life Lost (YPLL).

The ARDI on a yearly average account for 95,158 deaths caused by excessive alcohol consumption. That works out to be 261 deaths per day. The YPLL on a yearly average account for the loss of 29 years of individuals who drink excessive amounts of alcohol with certain diseases. In total, 2.8 million lost years because of the link between excessive consumption of alcoholics with certain diseases each year, which constitutes a tragedy in itself.

A critical question is: how can you prevent the initial first drink of alcohol? Frances Jensen (Jensen 2015), who was a single mom raising two teenage boys always keeps her liquor cabinet locked. If one of her boys was going to a party at a friend's house, she always called the parents of the friend and asked if there was going to be an adult observer present and if they locked their liquor cabinets. She said that the parents of the friend always were pleasant and thankful for her concern.

As a bonus, I want to share another Medscape email I received on March 16, 2022. The author was Haelle, T, (2022) and the title of the paper was, *"Just One Extra Drink a Day May Change the Brain."* Researchers in the United Kingdom examined functional MRI brain scans from 36,678 healthy adults, ages 40 to 69, and compared those findings to the participants' weekly alcohol consumption. As a person's alcoholic intake increased, their gray matter and white matter volume decreased, getting worse the more weekly drinks they had. You can read this report at: <https://www.medscape.com/viewarticle/970355_print>

What follows now is the most important take-home message of this book. Now that you have looked at the figures of the CT brain scans comparing the alcoholic and drug user brains to the non-alcoholic brains, you can understand how the 40 years employed CT technician in

Valdosta, Georgia can easily identify who has a non-alcoholic brain by just glancing at the CT brain scan.

Another name for alcohol is 'toxic ethanol', which is a small molecule capable of penetrating the Blood-Brain-Barrier and destroying both gray matter and white matter. The brains of chronic alcoholics gradually deteriorate to the extent that the chronic alcoholics find it difficult to learn new things, lose memory, find it difficult to make decisions, lose self-confidence, and become depressed and despondent. But, if the alcoholic completely stops drinking alcohol, like a miracle the tiny granular neurons in the hippocampus turn into neuronal stem cells and are capable of returning the brain back to normal. The key factor appears to be that chronic alcoholic consumption did not go on for too long.

So, your job (if you chose to take it) is to tell everybody you see that chronic alcoholism can destroy your brain, but, if you stop consumption completely, you can restore your brain completely back to normal. Tell all the kids you see that alcohol can ruin the only brain they will ever have. The imperative is that the fact that chronic alcoholism destroys the brain and this should become common knowledge for everybody on earth to people of all ages. So, everyone should spread the word to everyone they see.

Chapter Eight
Epilogue

The prologue describes my introduction to the fact that chronic alcoholics and drug addicts have distorted brains, missing significant parts of both gray matter and white matter following long-term consumption of alcohol and/or addicting drugs. There is a brief section on my public health experience and research interest, as well as, those funding agencies that supported my published research. It mentions my own addiction to cigarettes and my association with family alcoholics.

In chapter two, after digging deep into the literature, going to AA meetings, talking with family members of alcoholics, and remembering incidents from my childhood, I came up with a new idea of how to catch the attention of alcoholics and non-alcoholics alike, featuring a program to make the damaged brains to be actively advertised for all to know and be aware of, as the major deterrent to prevent adolescents from that first alcoholic drink. It is better to emphasize the truth openly than to meekly merely mention quietly the dangers of a distorted brain. Also, the lack of knowledge about the present status of brain damage, makes one wonder, if the liquor industry, is not using the same playbook as the tobacco industry in the 1950s when they had advertised doctors saying that nicotine was not a health problem.

In chapter three, I reported on what it was like growing up with the likes of a useless alcoholic with the turmoil and uncertainty that constantly prevailed. Also, I mentioned how my older brother and I ran away finally to go meet our biological father who basically was a super nice guy, except when provoked by his alcoholic wife.

Chapter four was filled with useful statistics and cost factors of AUD as reported by WHO, NIH, CDC, and certain foundations. The progressive pathological process was followed from Wernicke's encephalography to the Wernicke-Korsakoff syndrome (wet brain), and the culmination of the severe damage to both the gray matter and white matter by the use of CT and MRI scans. Not only does alcohol restrict the absorption of thiamin leading consequently to the death of neurons, but alcohol itself can also result in the death of neurons. The good news is: the discovery of neurogenesis, the glymphatic system, and the shrinking of glial elements are all interrelated and raise the possibility of providing improved treatments for certain types of brain diseases in the future.

In chapter five, I revealed my susceptibility to peer pressure by starting to smoke, when there really was not a good reason to begin doing that in the first place. I rigidly followed the steps outlined in a book on how to stop smoking during a summer vacation but relapsed in the fall semester with the stress of the first test in veterinary school. This exact sequence of events re-occurred the very next summer vacation and with the first fall semester test pressure and stress. In the last summer vacation of veterinary school, my foolish pride forced me to not give in to my boss's insistence that I quit smoking. However, seeing the comparison of nice smooth pink lungs of a non-smoker, next to the black wrinkled lungs of a smoker at the medical school pathology exhibit in San Francisco convinced me never to ever smoke again (except for one day in India as outlined in an excerpted story from one of my previous books). Perhaps the greatest surprise to me was the feeling of freedom from the control that my addiction had over me. The craving for a cigarette controlled my time and became so inhibiting to my schedule of what I really wanted to do, it seemed like I was held hostage.

Once I stopped smoking, I became more self-confident, inquisitive, and happy. It is terrible to realize that you have no control over your own brain and there is no control over taking drugs to solve your craving for items that you know deep down are poison and threaten your very existence, but you are hopeless to stop. After one experience at an AA meeting, I asked one of the alcoholics, "Here, let me show you what your brain scan looks like," as I took out my cell phone ready to tap the 'gallery' icon.

He answered, "I don't care about that at all. I just want to try and stay alive."

The young man that led that particular AA meeting, who looked like he was maybe 16 or 17 years old, admitted to the group that he had tried to commit suicide three times unsuccessfully.

One of my half-sisters told me after our sister Chrissy died of alcoholism, that when Chrissy was just a baby, she had been seen on multiple occasions crawling across the carpet on the living room floor where they lived to open the doors of the liquor cabinet and play with the half empty bottles of alcohol. Nobody knows for sure when Chrissy took her first drink of alcohol. Parents of young children should keep their alcohol under lock and key for the sake of their children's future, so they will have a future worth living.

The 18th Amendment to the United States Constitution which established the prohibition of alcohol in the United States was a dismal failure (the only amendment that has ever been repealed). Its failure almost suggests that everyone that has children, should pass a test to determine if they are knowledgeable enough to drink alcohol responsibly so as not to endanger their children's lives.

They say today (whoever they are) that alcohol is not all bad. That it makes some timid people more sociable and relaxed in gathering and relieves stress, among other unsubstantiated claims of benefits.

Below I have presented the words of Robert G. Ingersoll, one of the most celebrated orators and free thinkers (an agnostic) of the nineteenth century. Early in his career, he sent a bottle of bourbon to his prospective son-in-law with the following letter attached: *"I send you some of the most wonderful whiskey that ever drove the skeleton from a feast or painted landscape in the brain of man. It is mingled souls of wheat and corn. In it you will find the sunshine and the shadow that chased each other over the billowy fields; the breath of June; the carol of the lark; the dews of the night; the wealth of summer and the autumn's rich content, all golden with imprisoned light. Drink it and you will hear the voices of men and maidens singing the*

'Harvest Home', mingled with the laughs of children. Drink it and you will feel within your blood the star-lit dawns, the dreamy, tawny dusks of many perfect days. For forty years, this liquid joy has been within the happy staves of oak, longing to touch the lips of men."

Now read his assessment of alcohol following apparently many years of maturity: *"I am aware that there is a prejudice against any man engaged in the manufacture of alcohol. I believe, from the time it issues from the coiled and poison worm in the distilleries until it enters into the hell of death, dishonor, and crime, that it – from its source to where it ends. I do not believe anybody can contemplate the subject without becoming prejudiced against the liquid crime. All we have to do is to think of the wrecks on either side of the stream of the suicides, of the insanity, of the ignorance, of the destitution produced by the devilish thing. And when you think of the jails, of the almshouses, of the asylums, of the scaffolds upon either bank, I do not wonder that every thoughtful man is prejudiced against the damned stuff called alcohol."*
(<http://www.straightboubon.com/community/topic/10900 -a-quip-from-robert-ingersoll-on-whiskey>)

Now I will tell you what I do know in less glib language based on my personal experience. Alcohol kills many alcoholics but also kills many innocent people, not only on the highways but by sapping the joys of life from caregivers frustrated by the alcoholics' inability to demonstrate rational thinking. This inability to express rational thinking is mainly caused by the action of alcohol destroying significant portions of both the gray matter and white matter of the human brain. This destruction of gray matter and white matter is easily recognized by anyone looking at a CT brain scan and this fact should be taught to all grade school, middle school, junior high school, senior high school, and college students throughout the country. It is my fervent wish that somehow I will be able to act as a catalyst to spread the word by all means available. Thank you, dear reader, for getting this far in the book, and please tell your friends and family about its central message that alcohol can ruin your life because it can and does ruin your brain.

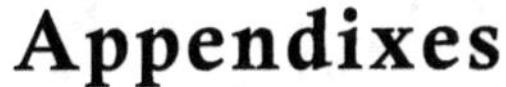
Appendixes

Appendix A: Abbreviations

AA	Alcoholics Anonymous
AQP-4	Aquaporin-4
ARDI	Alcohol-Related Disease Impact
AUD	Alcohol Use Disorde
BBB	Blood-Brain-Barrier
BrdU	BromodeoxyUridine
cAMP	cyclic Adenosine Mono Phosphate
CDC	Center for Disease Control and Prevention
CNN	Cable News Network
CNS	Central Nervous System
CPA	Certified Public Accountant
CREB	Clean Renewable Energy Bond
CSF	Cerebral Spinal Fluid
CT	Computed Tomography
FDA	Food and Drug Administration
DNA	Deoxyribonucleic Acid
LSD	Lysergic Acid Diethylamide
MOMP	Mitochondrial Outer Membrane Permeabilization
MRI	Magnetic Resonance Imaging
NGO	Non-Government Organization

NIAAA	National Institute of Alcohol, Abuse, and Alcoholism
NIH	National Institute of Health
NSC	Neurogenic Stem Cell
PNS	Peripheral Nervous System
ROS	Reactive Oxygen Species
YPLL	Years of Potential Life Lost
WHO	World Health Organization

Appendix B: Glossary

ADDICTION = The state of being compulsively committed to a habit or practice or to something that is psychologically or physically habit-forming, such as narcotics, to such an extent that its cessation causes severe trauma.

ANGSTROM = A unit of length, equal to one-tenth of a millimicron, or one ten-millionth of a millimeter.

APOPTOSIS = A process of programmed cell death in multicellular organisms.

ASTROCYTES = A star-shaped neuroglial cell of ectodermal origin.

ATAXIC = Loss of coordination of the muscles, especially of the extremities.

ATROPHY = A degeneration, or decline, as from disuse.

BLOOD-BRAIN-BARRIER = a network of blood vessels that is made up of closely spaced cells and helps to keep harmful substances from entering the brain.

CANKER SORE = An ulceration of a mucous membrane, especially of the mouth.

CARCINOGEN = Any substance or agent that tends to produce cancer.

COMPUTED TOMOGRAPHY = Computerized Axial Tomography (CAT) or (Abbreviated, simply "CT").

CONFABULATION = The replacement of a gap in a person's memory by falsification of what he or she believes to be true.

CNS = Central Nervous System.

DEMENTIA = Severe impairment or loss of intellectual capacity and personality integration, due to the loss of, or damage to neurons in the brain.

DENTATE GYRUS = One of the two interlocking gyri composing the hippocampus.

ENCEPHALOGRAPHY = The branch of medical science concerned with taking and analyzing X-ray photographs of the brain.

FORAMEN MAGNUM = The large opening in the base of the skull forms the passage from the cranial cavity to the spinal canal.

GLIAL CELLS = Any of the cells making up the neuroglia, especially the astrocytes, oligodendroglia, and microglia.

GLYMPHATIC SYSTEM = Recently (2013) discovered a system that removes daily waste products of the CNS in vertebrates.

GRAY MATTER = The gray tissue of the brain and spinal cord containing nerve cell bodies, dendrites, and bare (unmyelinated) axons.

HIPPOCAMPUS = An enfolding of the cerebral cortex into the lateral fissure of a cerebral hemisphere, having a major role in learning, emotion, and memory, and named for the seahorse shape of its cross-section.

IN SITU = Situated in the original, natural, or existing place or position, undisturbed.

IN VITRO = (of a biological process) made to occur in a laboratory vessel or other controlled experimental environment rather than within a living organism or natural setting.

IN VIVO = (of a biological process) occurring or made to occur within a living organism or natural setting.

LAMELLA = A thin plate, membrane, or layer of tissue or cell wall.

LOCUS COERULEUS = A bluish reticular nucleus in the central gray area of the caudal midbrain and part of the reticular formation. Its output axons project widely and diffusely to all parts of the CNS. Signals from the locus coeruleus appear to enhance the overall attentiveness level of the brain.

LYSERGIC ACID DIETHYLAMIDE = (LSD) A powerful psychedelic drug that produces temporary hallucinations and a schizophrenic psychotic state.

METABOLISM = The sum of the physical and chemical processes in an organism by which its material substance is produced, maintained, and destroyed, and by which energy is made available.

MICROGLIAL CELLS = Are non-neuronal cells forming part of the adventitial structure of the CNS. They are migratory and act as phagocytes of waste products of the nervous system.

MYELIN = Soft, white, fatty material produced by Schwann cells in the PNS and oligodendroglia cells in the CNS to cover axons.

NEUROTRANSMITTERS = Any of several chemical substances, such as epinephrine or acetylcholine, that transmit nerve impulses across a synapse to a postsynaptic element, or another nerve, muscle, or gland.

NOREPINEPHRINE = A neurotransmitter released by adrenergic nerve terminals in the autonomic nerve system and the CNS, that has such effects as constricting blood vessels, raising blood pressure, and dilating bronchi (also called noradrenaline).

OLIGODENDROGLIAL CELLS = The glial cells that form the myelin sheath around the axons of the neurons in the CNS.

PARENCHYMA = The specific tissue of an animal organ as distinguished from its connective or supporting tissues.

PERI-ARTERIOLAR SPACE = A recently discovered space surrounding large arteries in the cerebral nervous system that can expand or contract to allow the CSF to clean the adjacent extra-cellular interstitial spaces of trash via the glymphatic system.

PERI-VENOUS SPACE = A recently discovered space surrounding large veins in the cerebral nervous system that can expand or contract, so as to collect the trash from the glymphatic system to eventually exit the skull via the veins passing from the foramen magnum.

PNS = Peripheral Nervous System.

PONS = A band of nerve fibers in the brain connecting the lobes of the midbrain, medulla, and cerebrum.

PSYCHOSIS = A mental disorder characterized by symptoms, such as delusions or hallucinations that indicate impaired contact with reality.

SCHWANN CELLS = It is the cell in the peripheral nervous system that wraps around a nerve fiber, jelly-roll fashion forming the myelin sheath.

SUBGRANULAR ZONE (SV) = It is a brain region in the hippocampus where adult neurogenesis occurs. The other site of neurogenesis is the subventricular zone in the brain.

SUBVENTRICULAR ZONE (SVZ) = It is a region situated on the outside of each lateral ventricle in vertebrates. Neuronal Stem Cells reside there.

WET BRAIN = It is the informal name for the Wernicke – Korsakoff Syndrome, which is a type of brain disease caused by undue alcohol consumption.

WHITE MATTER = It is nerve tissue, especially of the brain and spinal cord, which primarily contains myelinated fibers and is nearly white in color.

Appendix C: References

Amini, S. et al. 2009 "p38SJ, a Novel DINGG Protein Protects Neuronal Cells from Alcohol Induced Injury and Death." J. Cell Physiol. 221 (3): 499–504; DOI 10.1002/jcp.21903

Amthor, F. 2016 "Neuroscience for Dummies," 2nd Edition. John Wiley & Sons, Hoboken, NJ. 379 pages.

Anonymous Diary, 1999 "Go Ask Alice."

Antonio, AM, Druse, MJ, 2008, "Antioxidants prevent ethanol-associated apoptosis in fetal rhombencephalic neurons." Brain Res. 1204:16–23.

Asklistenlearn: "Kids and Alcohol Don't Mix." 2003. (Foundation for Alcohol Responsibility [responsibility.org]). Arlington, VA.

Badaut, J. et al. 2002 Review Article; "Aquaporins in Brain: Distribution, Physiology, and Pathophysiology," J. Cerebral Blood Flow & Metabolism 22:367–378.

Benga, G. 2015 "The First Discovered Water Channel Protein, Later Called Aquaporin 1: Molecular Characteristics, functions, and Medical Implications," Review Mol Aspects Med. 33 (5–6): 18–34.

Benveniste, H. 2019 "The Glymphatic System and Clearance with Brain Aging: A review." Gerontology 65, no, 2 <Karger.com/article/fulltext/490349>

Buddy, T. 2020 "What is Alcohol Use Disorder." <Verywellmind.com/what-is-alcohol-abuse-63273>

Buddy, T. 2021 "Economic Impact of Alcohol Abuse in the U.S.: How Alcoholism and Binge Drinking Hits All of Our Wallets."
<https://www.verywellmind.com/the-cost-of-excessive-alcohol-use-in-the-U-S-67482>

Cala, L.A. et al. 1978 "Brain Atrophy and Intellectual Impairment in Heavy drinkers: a Clinical, psychometric Computerized Tomography Study." Aust. NZ J. Med. 8: 147–153; DOI 10.1111/J.445-5994.tb04502.x

Carter, R. 2019 "The Human Brain," 3rd Ed. Penguin Random House, London, 264 pages. bwc/news/article/the-cleab

Cherry, K. 2020 "Does Drinking Alcohol Kill Brain Cells?" <verywellmind.com/Does-Drinking-Alcohol-kill-Brain-Cells-2794887>. Accessed Sept. 19, 2021.

CNN Report: "Government not spending much on drug prevention." May 28, 2009.
<edition.cnn.com/2009/health/05/28/addiction.costs/>

DK 2020 "How the Brain Works: The Facts Visually Explained." Penguin Random House, NY. 324 pages.

Eagleman, D. 2015 "The Brain: The Story of You." Canongate, London. 246 pages.

Eriksson, P.S. et al. 1998. "Neurogenesis in the adult Human Hippocampus." Nature Medicine 4:1313–1317. DOI 10.1038/3305

Esser, M. B., Adam, S., Liu, Y. et al. 2020. "Death and Years of Potential Life Lost from Excessive Alcohol Use – United States 2011–2015." CDC Morbidity Mortality Weekly Report, October 2, 2020/69(39); 1428–1433.

Faust, F. 2019. "The Cleansing Power of a Deep Night's Sleep."
<dept.Washington.edu/mbwc/news/article/the-cleansing-of-a-deep-nights-sleep>

Fortier, C.B. 2014. News Release 18-Nov-2014 "Chronic alcohol intake can damage white matter pathways across the entire brain." Alcoholism Clinical & Experimental Research. https://eurekalert.org/news-release/902510.

French, M.D, et al. 2008. "The Economic Costs of Substance Abuse Treatment: Updated Estimates and Cost

Bands for Program Assessment and Reimbursement." J. Subst. Abuse Treat. Dec. 35(4) 462–469.

Fuchs, E. and Gould, E. 2000. Mini-Review: "In Vivo Neurogenesis in the Adult Brain: Regulations and functional implications." Europ. J. of Neuroscience. 12:2211–2214.

Griel, J. 2019. "Never Enough: The Neuroscience and Experience of Addiction." Doubleday, NY 233 pages.

Healle, T. 2022. "Just One Extra Drink a Day May Change the Brain" – Medscape – Mar 16, 2022 <https://www.medscape.com/viewarticle/970355_print>

Hammond, D. et al. 2006. "Effectiveness of Cigarette Warning Labels in Informing Smokers about the Risks of Smoking: Findings from the International Tobacco Control (ITC) Four Country Survey." Tab. Control 2006 Jan. 15 (Suppl. 3) iii19-iii25. DOI 10.1136/tc.2005.012294

Haorah, J, Ramirez, SH, Floveani, N. Gorantla, S, Morsey, B, Persidsky, Y. 2008, "Mechanism of alcohol-induced oxidative stress and neuronal injury." Free Radic Biol Med. 45:1542–1550.

Harper, C. 2009. "The neuropathology of Alcohol-related Brain Damage." Alcohol & Alcoholism 44: 136–140.

Harper, C.G. and Blumberg, P.C. 1982. "Brain Weights in Alcoholics." J. Neuro Neurosurg. Psychiatry 45: 838–840.

Hawkins, J.D. et al. 2002. "Promoting Science-Based Prevention in Communities." Addictive Behaviors 27(6) November–December 2002, Pages 951–976.

Heaton, MB, Paiva, M, Mayer, J, Miller, R, 2002. "Ethanol-mediated generation of reactive oxygen species in developing rat cerebellum." Neurosci Lett. 334:83–86.

Heaton, MB, Paiva, M, Madorsky, I, Mayer, J, Moore, DB, 2003. "Effects of ethanol on neurotrophic factors, apoptosis-related proteins, endogenous antioxidants, and reactive oxygen species in neonatal striatum: relationship to periods of vulnerability," Dev Brain Res. 140:237–252.

Heshmat, S. 2018. "The Role of Denial in Addiction: Denial is a Key Obstacle to Recovery." Psychology Today. Nov. 13, 2018.

Hollville, E. et al. 2019 "Apoptotic Cell Death Regulations in Neurons." Febs 286 issue 17, Sept. 2019 pages 3276–3298, DOI 10.1111/febs.14970

Hoyumpa, A.M. Jr. "Mechanism of Thiamin Deficiency in Chronic Alcoholism." Amer. Journal of Clinical Nutrition 33(12), 2750–2761.

Jensen, F. E. and Nutt, A. E. 2015. "The Teenage Brain: A Neuroscientist's Survival Guide to Raising Adolescents and Young Adults." HarperCollins, NY. 372 pages.

Jessen, N.A. et al. 2015. "The Glymphatic System – A Beginners Guide." Neurochem. Res. 40(12) 2583–2599. DOI: 10.1007/s11064-015-1581-6

Kesner, R.P. 2018. "An Analysis of Dentate Gyrus Function (an Update)." Behavioral Brain Research 354:84–91. DOI 10.1016/jbbr.2017.07.033

Komro, K.A. and Toomey, T.L. 2002. "Strategies to Prevent Underage Drinking." Alcohol Research and Health 26(1): 5–14.

Lee, JH, Tajuddin, NF, Le, PT, Druse, MJ, 2007. "A serotonin-1A agonist provides protection against the ethanol-induced decrease of endogenous antioxidant enzymes in fetal rhombencephalic neurons." Alcohol Clin Exp Res. 31:37A.

Martin, P.R. et al. 2003. "The Role of Thiamin Deficiency in Alcohol Brain Disease," Alcohol Research & Health. 27(2): 124–142.

Mate, G. 2010. "In The Realm of Hungry Ghosts: Close Encounters with Addiction." North Atlantic Books 536 pages.

Nagelhus, E.A. and Ottersen, O.R. 2013. "Physiological Roles of Aquaporin-4 in Brain." Physiol. Rev. Oct. 93940: 1543–1562.

Nedergaard, M. 2015. "Cleaning the Brain Prevents Dementia." Health and Medical Sciences. <Health Sciences.Ku.dk/about/excellent-University of Copenhagen research/Majken-Nedergaard>

Nowinski, J. 2021. "Preventing Teen Substance Abuse." Psychology Today. Aug. 3, 2021. <psychologytoday.com/intl/blog/the-almost-effect/202108/preventing-teen-substance-abuse>

NIAAA 2021. "Alcohol Facts and Statistics, June 2021." <NIAAA.NIH.gov/publications/brochures-and-facts-sheets/alcohol-facts-and statistics>

NIAAA 2006. "Underage Drinking: Alcohol Alert No. 67."

NIAAA 2007. "Alcohol Alert No. 72." <pubs.niaaa.nih.gov/publications/aa72/aa72.htm>

O'Donnell, J. et al. 2015. "Distinct Functional States of Astrocytes During Sleep and Wakefulness: Is Norepinephrine the Master Regulator?" Curr. Sleep Med. Rep. March 1(1): 1–8.

O'Malley, G.F. and O'Malley, R. 2020. "Korsakoff Psychosis." <msdmanual.com/en-au/professional/special-subjects/recreational-drugs-and-intoxicants/Korsakoff-psychosis>

Patel, S, et al. 2018. "Wernicke Encephalopathy" Cures 10(8):e3187 DOI 10.7759/cureus 3187

Pompili, M. et al. 2010. "Suicidal Behavior and Alcohol Abuse." Int. J. Environ. Res. Public Health 7(4) 1392–1431. doi: 10.3390/ijerph7041392

Ramachandran, V, Watts, LT, Maffi, SK, Chen, J, Schenker, S, Henderson, G, 2003. "Ethanol-induced oxidative stress precedes mitochondrially mediated apoptotic death of cultured fetal neurons." J Neurosci Res, 74:577–588.

Rostron, C. 2019. "The Science Behind Why We Drink Alcohol" The Open University 30 Aug. 2019.

Rice and Chen Gu 2019. "Function and mechanism of Myelin Regulation in Alcohol and Alcoholism." Bioassays Jul. 41(7) e1800255.

Reynolds, B.A. and Weiss, S. 1992. "Generation of Neurons and Astrocytes from Isolated Cells of the Adult Mammalian Central Nervous System." Science 255:1707–1710.

Ridley, N.J. et al. 2013. "Alcohol-Related Dementia: An Update of the Evidence." Alz Res Therapy 5, 3 DOI 10.1186/alzrt157.

Stony Brook University 2015. "Could Body Posture During Sleep Affect How Your Brain Cleans Waste?" Aug. 4,

2015.
<Sciencedaily.com/releases/2015/08/150804203440.htm>

<sites.duke.edu/apep/module-2-the-abcs-of-intoxication/content/alcohol-to-the-brain-crossing-blood-brain-barrier>

Sandhu, G.S. and Nagrale, H.R. 2020. "Computed Tomography Evaluation of Brain in Chronic Alcoholics." Neuro sci. Rural Pract. 11(1): 063–071.

Takata, K. 2004. "Aquaporins: Water Channel Protein of the Cell Membrane." Prog Histochem Cytechem 39(1):1–83. DOI 10.1016/J.proghi.2004.03.001.

Tate, P. and Ellis, A. 1997. "Alcohol: How to Give it Up, and Be Glad You Did." Sharp Press; 1731 Tucson, AZ 85702–1731 228 pp.

Tateno, M. and Saito, T. 2008 "Biological Studies on Alcohol-Induced Neuronal Damage." Psychiatry Investig. Mar. 5(1) 21–23.

Thomson, A.D. 2000. "Mechanism of Vitamin Deficiency in Chronic Alcohol Misusers and the Development of the Wernicke-Korsakoff Syndrome." Alcohol and Alcoholism: 35 (suppl):2–7.

Vasan, S. and Kumar, A. 2020. "Wernicke Encephalography." Stat Pearls Treasure Island, FL, Stat Pearls Publ. 2021 Jan.

Walker, M. 2017. "Why We Sleep." Simon and Schuster, Digital Sales Inc.

Watson, J. 2021. "Moderate Alcohol's Health Benefits Look Increasingly Doubtful." Medscape Medical News, December 25, 2021. Email received by Stewart Odendhal.

Watts, LT, Rathinam, ML, Schenker, S, Henderson, GI, 2005. "Astrocytes protect neurons from ethanol-induced oxidative stress and apoptotic death." J Neurosci Res, 80:655–666.

Wernicke, C. 1881. "Der Acute Haemorrhasische Polioencephalitis Superior." Vol. 2 Kassel.
Zahr, N.M. and Pfefferbaum, A. 2017. "Alcohol's Effect on the Brain: Neuroimaging Results in Human and Animal Models." Alcohol Research 38(2): 183–206.

Appendix D:
Acknowledgements

In particular, I want to thank the two authors that wrote the Article which was entitled (Computed Tomography Evoluation of Brain in Chronic Alcoholics), which was written by G.S. Sandhu and H.R. Nagtale, in the Journal: J Neurosci Rural Pract 2020: 11:63–71; which was published by Geor Thieme Verlag Publisher, who provided the permission to us to use the CT Brain scan Figures in this book.

I wish to thank all of my family members, friends, and neighbors who expressed interest in this project and gave me encouragement during the process. In particular, Charles Joseph Odendhal, III, Baba Creelman, and her husband Bill, deserve gold stars for their editing and valuable suggestions. My lifelong friend Don Chery also provided several good ideas and suggestions that proved to be of value.

Appendix E: About the Author

Because his diverse research interests and financial support have taken him to many different parts of the world, he considers himself to be a planetary citizen. He and his wonderful wife, Marta, spend their summers in Prague, Czech Republic, and winters in Fort Lauderdale, Florida. They take cruises back and forth because they meet interesting people and there is no jet lag.

Education

1951–1955. Casady High School (Parochial College Prep-school); Oklahoma City, Oklahoma.

1955–1957. The University of the South; Sewanne, Tennesee.

1957–1060. UCLA. B.A.; Vertebrate Zoology.

1963–1967. University of California at Davis. DVM; Senior Class President and Citation for Outstanding Undergraduate Achievement in Anatomy.

1973–1977 The University of Missouri at Columbia. Ph.D. in Anatomy and Immunology from a joint study program with the Medical School and the Veterinary

School; Citation for Outstanding Graduate Student-teacher award 1975.

Employment:

1947: Barney Stewart Lumber. Operated the wholesale mailing room after school and also delivered the daily Advertiser Newspaper for three years. Other summer jobs during high school included being a soda jerk for a drugstore; unloading box cars at the freight yards at the lumber company, and working in a machine shop at W and W Steel Company.

At the University of the South, I stoked the coal furnace of the fraternity house and did not have to pay my monthly fraternity bill; I worked for the alumni office at the University and worked for the science department setting up and clearing up after the different experiments.

At UCLA, I was a "hasher" (someone who sets up the dining table for the meals, cleans up after the meals at the fraternity house, and in exchange, gets to eat the same food for free.) Then, from 6:00 pm to 10:00 pm I worked at the Texico Gas Station filling up people's vehicles with gas and as it was rarely busy, I could study my homework assignments easily most of the time. During my last semester, I worked from 6:00 pm to 11:00 pm in the Admitting Office of the Mount Sinai Hospital in Beverly Hills.

At UC, Davis, every Saturday I worked cleaning the cages of the animals and assisting in surgeries at the Land Park Veterinary Hospital for three years and I got paid $50 per month by a pet pharmaceutical company to distribute

101

their product information brochures and pamphlets to the veterinary faculty every once in a while.

1960–1961: Nicholas Proprietary Limited; Sydney, Australia. It was a pharmaceutical manufacturer and I called on doctors, dentists, and drugstores to promote the company's products.

1961–1961: I worked briefly as the night clerk at the Clift Hotel in Laguna Beach, California.

1961–1963: Burroughs-Welcome & Co. another pharmaceutical manufacturer. I was called a "detail man" because I gave all of the details of the company's products to doctors, dentists, and drugstores. Then, for my first summer vacation from veterinary school, the same company rehired me to work for them in the suburban communities south of Oakland, California.

1961–1965: I work on a sea lion project for the Stanford Research Institute part-time during school on weekends and full-time on the next summer vacation.

1966 (June to September): I was employed by the U.S. Fish and Wildlife Services to perform necropsies (similar to human autopsies) on dead fur seal pups on the Pribilof Island in the middle of the Bering Sea west of Alaska.

1967–1971: I was hired by the Department of Pathobiology at the School of Hygiene and Public Health at Johns Hopkins University to go to India and join a group of scientists studying foreign diseases that have never been seen in the United States before (funded by the NIH).

1971–1973: Pfizer Pharmaceutical Company, Terre Haute, Indiana. I was hired as a research veterinarian to conduct experiments to submit to the Food and Drug Administration (FDA) for clearance of new animal medications, which involved a great deal of travel throughout the U.S.

1973–1977: The University of Missouri at Columbia. I was hired to teach the veterinary student anatomy and histology and worked on my Ph.D. at the same time with a salary almost the same as Pfizer was paying me.

1977–1978: I received a competitive grant from the Indo-US Sub-Commission on Education and Culture to study Foot and Mouth disease in cattle and repeated similar studies I reported on from my Johns Hopkins work of 10 years before.

1978–1998: The University of Georgia in Athens, GA in the Department of Anatomy and Radiology. I also had a participation in the development of a Master's degree in Ecology at the Institute of Ecology and later became the Assistant Director of the Office of International Development in the University's higher administration.

1980: United States Department of Agriculture (USDA) Program to eradicate the epidemic of African swine fever in Haiti. The USDA spent $14 million to kill every single pig in Haiti and repopulate clean pigs afterward; because it was determined that if Haitian boat people might bring infected pig meat with them to the USA; and because of the long incubation period of the disease, it would cost the U.S. billions of dollars to fight the disease in the USA. So, I joined the USDA program along with other scientists and veterinarians from Mexico, Haiti, Dominican Republic, Texas, Florida, and Georgia to spend 4 months working in Haiti.

1981: I received a Senior Fulbright Research Award to determine if native and/or cross-bred cattle in India had evidence in their blood of the Bovine Leukosis Virus. Ten percent of both the native and cross-bred cattle demonstrated antibodies against the virus.

1986: I received a Second Senior Fulbright Award to study significant changes in the human and cattle populations over 20 years from my Johns Hopkins work in 1967–1971.

1987–1992: I received a multi-year competitive individual Grant from the National Academy of Sciences to study in China the change in agricultural ownership of cattle and other domestic animals at the village level.

1995–1998: I became the Director of the European Center of Georgia which was affiliated with the East-West Institute of New York City. Its main aim was to create cooperative ties between the major universities in the Southeastern United States and the recently liberated universities of Eastern Europe.

2008–2022: I was hired by the scientific journal *"Folia Veterinaria"* as the "Language Editor" to assist non-English speaking writers improve their English composition once their article was accepted for publication.

Publications (mostly in peer-reviewed scientific journals) = 64

Grants (to support my research) = 26

Presentations (invited, conventions, and conferences) = 59

Civic Activity and Public Service

1976–1977: President of the Central Missouri Humane Society.

1981–1982: President of Georgia Chapter of the Society for International Development.

1985–1987: President of Athens, GA Unitarian-Universalist Fellowship.

1992–1994: Co-Chair of Oconee County Clean and Beautiful Commission.

1994–1995: President of Kiwanis Club of Athens, GA.

1994–1995: Chairman of the Board of Directors of the Georgia Unit of the Recording for the Blind, Inc., in Athens, GA.

Honors and Awards

1963–1964: American Veterinary Medical Association/ class representative, re-elected 1964–1965.

1965–1966: Treasurer of Junior American Veterinary Medical Association, re-elected 1966–1967.

1966 Citation for Outstanding Undergraduate Achievement in Anatomy, University of California at Davis.

1973: Sigma Xi Honorary Society.

1975: Outstanding Graduate Student Teacher, University of Missouri.

1976: Nominated for Outstanding Young Man of America.

1977: Discovered a new species of nematode in the California sea lion, thus it was named after me, i.e., Dipetalonema Odendhali.

1977: Who's Who in the Midwest.

1977–1978: Indo-U.S. Sub-Commission on Education and Culture.

1979: Who's Who in the South and Southwest.

1979: Phi Zeta Honorary Society.

1980–1981: Senior Fulbright scholarship to India.

1986–1987: Senior Fulbright award to India.

1989–1998: Phi Beta Delta Honor Society for International Scholarship.

1992: Phi Beta Delta Faculty Award for Outstanding Scholarship, Leadership, and Service in the field of International Education.